T0374920

The Cincinnati Human Relations Commission

The
Cincinnati
Human
Relations
Commission

A History, 1943–2013

Phillip J. Obermiller and Thomas E. Wagner

Foreword by Michael E. Maloney

OHIO UNIVERSITY PRESS   ATHENS

Ohio University Press, Athens, Ohio 45701
ohioswallow.com
© 2017 by Ohio University Press

To obtain permission to quote, reprint, or otherwise
reproduce or distribute material from
Ohio University Press publications, please contact
our rights and permissions department at
(740) 593-1154 or (740) 593-4536 (fax).

Cover image: Cincinnati, Ohio from across the Ohio River.
Photo by Derek Jensen. Courtesy Wikimedia Commons.
Cover design by Beth Pratt.

Printed in the United States of America
Ohio University Press books are printed on acid-free paper ∞ ™

27 26 25 24 23 22 21 20 19 18 17   5 4 3 2 1

Library of Congress Cataloging-in-Publication Data
Names: Obermiller, Phillip J., author. | Wagner, Thomas E., author.
Title: The Cincinnati Human Relations Commission : a history, 1943-2013 /
  Phillip J. Obermiller, Thomas E. Wagner ; foreword by Michael E. Maloney.
Description: Athens : Ohio University Press, 2017. | Includes bibliographical
  references and index.
Identifiers: LCCN 2017026386| ISBN 9780821422991 (hardback) | ISBN
  9780821446218 (pdf)
Subjects: LCSH: Cincinnati Human Relations Commission--History. | Civil
  rights--Ohio--Cincinnati--History. | Minorities--Political
  activity--Ohio--Cincinnati--History. | Cincinnati (Ohio)--Social
  policy--History. | BISAC: HISTORY / United States / 20th Century. |
  POLITICAL SCIENCE / Political Freedom & Security / Civil Rights.
Classification: LCC JC599.U52 O46 2017 | DDC 323.09771/7809045--dc23
LC record available at https://lccn.loc.gov/2017026386

This book is dedicated to those,
past and present, determined to
"safeguard the rights of all citizens."

Contents

CONTENTS

Illustrations

Foreword

Understanding the history of the Cincinnati Human Relations Commission requires understanding the emergence of Cincinnati's entire civic structure. The city's civic institutions are rooted in the Progressive Era, which lasted from the 1890s well into the twentieth century. Progressivism included the following characteristics:

- An affirmation of urban life and the belief that whatever ails the city can be fixed through planning and good government. For Progressives and their descendants, intergroup relations was just another problem such as overcrowding, substandard housing, poor health conditions, street maintenance, or waste management. Each could be fixed through civic dialogue and the intentional efforts that emerge from trust. Perhaps the clearest example of Progressivism in the city is the United Way of Greater Cincinnati (formerly the Community Chest and Council), where all problems are considered amenable to solution through rational policies, skillful administration, and strict budget accountability. Another example is the Charter Committee of Greater Cincinnati, a local good-government group that initiated home rule, civil service, and community planning.

- The belief that action at the neighborhood level is essential to the physical and social health of the city.

- Recognition of the impulses that drive women and other minorities to seek recognition and inclusion in the life of the city.

- The impulse of noblesse oblige, which says people with education and wealth have both the right and the obligation to help shape the life of the community.

Although Progressivism produced many local benefits, it was not an unalloyed good at the national level. Many Progressives believed in the primacy of science, the state, and their own superiority, and so backed policies such as eugenics and immigration restriction. Nevertheless, the Cincinnati Human Relations Commission (CHRC) is the creation of the Progressives and their mid-twentieth-century successors. Some of its founders and later leaders have been associated with the Woman's City Club, the Charter Committee, and the Cincinnatus Association, for example. Some of the perennial tensions that beset the CHRC reflect the conflict between noblesse oblige and the popular impulse to organize into political parties. Because the CHRC is ultimately subject to the mayor and city council, these officials can either champion or try to eliminate the commission based on their ideology and political needs. Hence, some mayors and council members have tried to replace CHRC functions with projects of their own creation and control.

The CHRC not only has been influenced by Cincinnati's traditional civic leaders and their associations but is also the product of the civil rights movement of the mid-to-late twentieth century and of the African American leaders that movement brought forth. This book gives voice to their struggles, to their contributions, and to their allies of all political stripes. During the 1960s and 1970s the CHRC also drew energy from the new activism that emerged from Cincinnati's thriving neighborhood movement.

The CHRC is both a product of these movements and, in varying degrees, an incubator of new organizations such as Housing Opportunities Made Equal, the Urban Appalachian Council, and People Working Cooperatively. The commission has also nurtured local manifestations of the women's movement and the organizational efforts of the LGBTQ community, people with disabilities, and Hispanics. It has aided and been aided by the movement of Jews and Muslims for recognition and inclusion in the life of the city. Thus the CHRC is an integral part of the city's civic infrastructure. Put simply, over the years the commission has provided a doorway into city hall for groups in the community that have in one way or another been marginalized. Its internal and external conflicts reflect the tensions among the various impulses described above, most notably the clashes between self-made citizens, elected officials, and city elites.

With this background in mind it may be instructive to examine how the CHRC History Project got started, was implemented, and resulted in this volume. When Dr. Ericka King-Betts became executive director of the Cincinnati Human Relations Commission, in August 2012, she became curious about the agency's history. Who were its past directors and what was their legacy? she wondered. After being told there were dozens of CHRC file boxes stored floor to ceiling in an obscure room in City Hall, and later discovering another large cache of file boxes in a storage facility in a neighboring city, she decided it was time to act.

With the encouragement of Dr. King-Betts, I developed a proposal to recover the agency's history. It stated in part:

> For the past 70 years the Cincinnati Human Relations Commission (CHRC), preceded by the Mayor's Friendly Relations Committee (MFRC), has been a vital part of Cincinnati's social fabric. It has sought to ameliorate racial tensions and serve as a focal point for intergroup relations. It has served as an important incubator for emerging constituency groups, including Appalachians, women, LGBTQ advocates, and people with disabilities. It has also been present to celebrate the work of human rights leaders and to inspire new leadership.

The proposal went on to point out that "the compilation and organization of these materials will benefit the CHRC in assessing its past and working with city leadership to plan its program for the future."

Dr. King-Betts saw the project as enabling an understanding of what worked well for the agency and what did not, as well as providing insights into current community conditions and the CHRC's responses. Community funders agreed: project grants were provided by Christ Church Cathedral (Episcopal), the Murray and Agnes Seasongood Good Government Foundation, and the Stephen H. Wilder Foundation. The CHRC provided both monetary and in-kind support in the form of staff assistance and materials.

With this encouragement and financial support, I set about forming a group to carry out the CHRC History Project. The initial project team consisted of me serving as project director; Dr. James Carson, archivist; Jeffrey Crawford, librarian/data base manager; Jeffrey Dey, data consultant; and Geoffrey Daniels, University of Cincinnati intern. When Dr. Carson withdrew for health reasons, Dr. Fritz Casey-Leininger, head of the Community History program at the University of Cincinnati, became the project archivist. Nathan McGee, a University of Cincinnati graduate student in history, compiled the newspaper index and organized the eighty boxes of new material Dr. King-Betts had found and directed to the University of Cincinnati archives. Drs. Phillip Obermiller and Thomas Wagner agreed to write the history.

The team first set out to locate all repositories of materials relating to the Mayor's Friendly Relations Committee and the Cincinnati Human Relations Commission. Interviews with people who were a part of MFRC/CHRC history were conducted to supplement the written documentation. We also expanded the project to include an index of newspaper articles referencing the MFRC and the CHRC for the seventy-year period. We then developed a comprehensive database and finding aid, updated the agency's timeline, and subsequently produced the book you have in hand.

At times, team members felt like detectives. Some useful collections outside Cincinnati were identified. For example, the estate of MFRC director Marshall Bragdon selected Tulane University to house his papers, while the files of the Urban Appalachian Council, including material on the CHRC, were located at the Berea College Archives, in Kentucky. Locally, the Community Relations Collection at Hebrew Union College housed related material, as did the University of Cincinnati's Archives and Rare Books Library, and the Cincinnati History Library and Archives. Dr. King-Betts discovered a photo of Jackie Robinson holding a CHRC poster and Janet Smith's history of the first five years of the MFRC in one of the many boxes stored at City Hall. Marshall Bragdon's 1945–65 manuscript history of the agency was located by Obermiller and Wagner, as was the first CHRC director's controversial report on the 1967 riots. Finding these key documents added excitement to the project as we became convinced that, without our work, some of these materials might have been lost or remained undiscovered.

On behalf of the project team, I invite you to share our excitement as you consider the lessons the CHRC's history has to offer for the practice of human relations in the city and the nation.

Michael E. Maloney
CHRC History Project Director

Acknowledgments

Ericka King-Betts, CHRC Executive Director
James Carson, Archival Consultant
Charles F. Casey-Leininger, Historian*
Jeffery Crawford, E-Resources Cataloging and Database Management
    Specialist*
James DaMico, Curator of Photographs and Prints, Cincinnati
    History Library and Archives
Geoffrey Daniels, Graduate Research Assistant*
Jeffrey Dey, Data Consultant
Christine Schmid Engels, Archives Manager, Cincinnati History
    Library and Archives
Kevin Grace, Head and University Archivist*
Michael E. Maloney, Project Director
Nathan McGee, Graduate Research Assistant*
Danilo Palazzo, Director, School of Planning*
Suzanne Maggard Reller, Reference/Collections Librarian*
Claire Smittle, Librarian, Cincinnati History Library and Archives
Eira Tansey, Digital Archivist/Records Manager*
    *at the University of Cincinnati

COOPERATING INDIVIDUALS

Helen Black, wife of Judge Robert Black
Tedd Good, LGBTQ community activist
Rev. Robert Harris, advocate for disabled people
Charles Judd, civic leader
Rev. Damon Lynch II, civil rights leader
Scott McLarty, LGBTQ activist
David McPheeters, first CHRC executive director

ACKNOWLEDGMENTS

Cheryl Meadows, former CHRC executive director
Judith Bogart Meredith, former CHRC communications director
Rev. Arzell Nelson, former CHRC executive director
Susan Noonan, former CHRC acting executive director
Barbara Smitherman, civic leader
Marian Spencer, civil rights activist
Judge S. Arthur Spiegel, former CHRC board president
Louise Spiegel, former CHRC member
Sen. Cecil Thomas, former CHRC executive director

COOPERATING INSTITUTIONS

Cooperating institutions include the University of Cincinnati Archives and Rare Books Library, Berea College Library and Archives, the Cincinnati and Hamilton County Public Library, the Cincinnati History Library and Archives, the Klau Library at Hebrew Union College–Cincinnati, and the Amistad Research Center at Tulane University.

FUNDING

This publication was made possible by grants from the Murray and Agnes Seasongood Good Government Foundation, Christ Church Cathedral, and the Stephen H. Wilder Foundation. Additional support was provided by the Cincinnati Human Relations Commission.

Introduction

Enter the phrase *human relations* into a search engine and you will get millions of hits, almost all having to do with the corporate management of
employees. Check the phrase in a Merriam-Webster dictionary and the
first definition is: "A study of human problems arising from organizational and interpersonal relations (*as in industry*)" (emphasis added). The
Encyclopedia Britannica is more explicit. In entries under both *public administration* and *industrial relations,* the encyclopedia finds the origin of *human
relations* in the pioneering efforts of Elton Mayo in the 1930s to develop
ways to increase productivity at Western Electric's Hawthorne plant near
Chicago. That is not what this book is about.

The concept of human relations is often confused with race relations, social movements for civil rights, and international agreements
guaranteeing human rights. Human relations encompasses, but is not
limited to, considerations of race; for example, gender, sexual orientation, ethnicity, religion, region of origin, physical and mental capacity
are but a few of the other characteristics of concern in human relations.
Human rights and civil rights are most often matters of local, state, and
national laws as well as international agreements—violate these norms
and charges may be brought, courts convened, and sanctions carried
out on those convicted. Human relations does not involve accusations
under the law, tribunals, or the imposition of penalties.

Let there be no doubt that the field of human relations is closely
aligned with movements for human and civil rights. It is definitely a

thread in the braided efforts for social justice among groups such as African Americans, women, Hispanics, and former felons, as well as LGBTQ, Jewish, Islamic, and indigenous people. There is clearly great overlap between human relations and the issues identified and acted upon by these and other groups. But there is a lot of confusion as well.

When the concepts of justice and rights are propounded in Western society the law is usually invoked as the arbiter of the outcomes being sought. Laws are established through political processes that distribute power in the social arena. Human relations is cognizant of, but does not directly concern itself with, the law, politics, or power.

Human relations is the endeavor to improve the social and inter-personal interactions among people, or simply put, to promote civility. It operates not in the realm of force or power or legal coercion, but in the realm of ethics, that is, the set of principles that govern a person's or a group's behavior. It operates best at the local level, from the bottom up, and complements larger-scale, top-down efforts to compel human behavior through legislation. Put bluntly, laws cannot change personal bias, prejudice, or bigotry. This is where the hard work of human rela-tions occurs, in affecting thinking and beliefs that are often expressed in behavior. To the extent that beliefs and behaviors are changed, human relations is a secular moral endeavor to help people distinguish between socially good and bad opinions and, just as important, actions.

Beyond civility, understanding, and good will, however, lie structural problems that must also be addressed, chiefly in the areas of employ-ment, housing, education, law enforcement, and public access (recre-ation, entertainment, dining, governmental programs, and so on). In his insightful essay "Whither Northern Race Relations Committees?" Robert Weaver writes, "It is often suggested that the Negro should lift himself by his own bootstraps, but it is usually forgotten that his feet are set in concrete. The first steps must be aimed at breaking the concrete. If a community is taking actions to improve the status of its Negro citizens, it is making the most effective contribution toward changing attitudes and behavior patterns." These words were written in 1944, following the devastation of the Detroit race riots, just as municipal human and race relations committees were being set up in cities across the country, including Cincinnati.

This is why the Cincinnati Mayor's Friendly Relations Committee (MFRC) was founded. It brought together a large number of citizens with a wide spectrum of beliefs with the goal of using persuasion to get different groups in the city to interact with mutual respect. The committee itself provided the public with role models for cooperative behavior, along with research and educational projects meant to document adverse conditions affecting various groups in the city, and to show how they can be changed.

The MFRC was replaced by the Cincinnati Human Relations Commission (CHRC) in the 1960s, reflecting the rapid change in social relations that occurred during that decade. While some other municipal human-relations agencies moved into enforcement during this era, the CHRC remained true to its human-relations roots while becoming more involved in youth-oriented programs and establishing neighborhood contact through a cadre of field-workers.

Over a seventy-year history, first the Mayor's Friendly Relations Committee then the Cincinnati Human Relations Commission have been emblematic of human-relations efforts across the nation. The agency has struggled to stay true to its own philosophy while adapting to social change, to use suasion in a culture that demands immediate and measurable results, and to operate effectively despite local political struggles. The history of the CHRC is a significant narrative within the larger civil rights movement and in the urban history of twentieth-century America. The CHRC's story is not one of unmitigated success but one of persistence through missteps and sometimes outright failures. Recounting the CHRC's history is not meant to valorize the commission but to document both its successes and disappointments; in doing so we acknowledge what a seemingly impossible yet necessary task improving urban human relations is. That is what this book is about.

METHOD

Throughout the volume we use the "posthole" method of historiography by focusing on themes we consider important for understanding the agency. Hundreds of boxes of archival materials spread across five libraries in three states make for some interesting reading, but we have condensed much of it for the sake of clarity and accessibility. Direct quotes from these records, reports, newsletters, speeches, memos, correspondence, and newspaper articles are presented to provide the reader with a first-person perspective; to the same end, the text includes portions of both archival and contemporary interviews with former MFRC and CHRC board and staff members. These methodological and format decisions are complemented by the detailed timeline provided in the appendices—history is made of many stories and the reader may find other compelling stories emerging from the timeline.

ORGANIZATION

This volume has been written and organized with the general reader in mind. A short preface in italics opens each chapter, summarizing selected local and national milestones (acts of Congress, executive orders, Supreme Court decisions, protests, and riots) that provide context for events in the nation and in Cincinnati that affected the agency's actions.

Although footnotes have not been used in the text, an extensive list of the sources consulted in developing the manuscript has been appended for scholarly use. The volume flows in chronological order, each chapter describing a decade in the work of the MFRC or the CHRC. Within each chapter, however, the narrative may reference past or future events in the agency's experience to show the interrelatedness of these circumstances. Photographs are presented to put faces on names and to highlight specific events.

The conclusion provides a broad perspective on Cincinnati's human relations efforts, placing them in the context of the American civil rights movement, relating them to similar efforts across the nation and pointing to the key role leadership played in these endeavors. In this light, the story of the CHRC becomes a case study illustrating the value of having a subtle but insistent voice for social justice within municipal government.

PJO
TEW
Cincinnati

1

Responding to the "Calamity in Detroit"

The 1940s

Popular belief notwithstanding, common threats such as economic downturns and external enemies did not fully unite Americans, nor did they calm ethnic, labor, or racial hostility in the United States during the twentieth century. Italians were lynched until at least 1915, Mexicans and Chinese through the 1930s, and blacks well into the 1960s. Growing ethnic antagonism resulted in severe immigration restriction laws being enacted in the early 1920s. In an effort "to preserve the ideal of American homogeneity," federal legislation was passed to cap the numbers of Southern and Eastern European as well as African immigrants to this country; Arabs and people from East Asia and India were excluded altogether. During the 1930s anti-Semitism in the United States limited German-Jewish immigration to a mere fraction of the allotted quota, with tragic results.

In similar fashion, labor unrest often led to battles among workers and between workers and employers, some of them deadly enough to be called massacres. Between 1900 and 1999 only thirteen individual years passed without notable, often bloody, strikes in the agricultural, mining, and manufacturing sectors.

Racial conflict was also widespread. Where Jim Crow did not prevail, the Ku Klux Klan and vigilantism did. Race riots occurred throughout the century, including during the First and Second World Wars. During the Second World War, for instance, there were hundreds of major strikes, some of them to protest the hiring of black workers in defense industries. By instituting a federal Fair Employment Practice Commission, in 1941, President Franklin Roosevelt narrowly averted a march on Washington by blacks protesting discriminatory defense industry hiring practices. In addition to protests by or about blacks, the century also saw anti-Greek, Hispanic/Latino, Puerto Rican, and Filipino riots. Clearly then, wars, a long period of economic depression, or intervals of prosperity and industrial growth never completely united Americans as a people.

In response to widespread prejudice and discrimination, resistance and advocacy groups sprang up throughout the twentieth century. They included the National Association for the Advancement of Colored People (1909), the National Urban League (1910), the Jewish Anti-Defamation League (1913), and more recently the Student Nonviolent Coordinating Committee (1960), the Irish American Cultural Institute (1962), the National Organization for Women (1966), the National Italian American Foundation (1975), the Human Rights Campaign (founded in 1980 as the Human Rights Campaign Fund, focusing on the election of candidates willing to treat LGBTQ issues equitably), and the American Association of People with Disabilities (1995) to name only a few. Although these dates would imply a period of quiescence through midcentury, this was not the case. For instance, the Congress of Racial Equality was founded in 1942 and the Southern Christian Leadership Conference in 1957.

Just as important, another thread of state and local activism, sometimes called the Civic Unity Movement, began to appear. Writing in 1951, the director of the Center for Human Relations Studies in New York, Dan W. Dodson, noted,

> *It was clear that the [Second World War] had forced a showdown on the second-class citizenship status of Negro citizens. It was also clear that in addition to the national aspect of the issue, it was also a community problem. Another revelation was the fact that municipal governments were woefully unprepared and inexperienced either to understand the problem or to deal with it. These conditions led to a new instrumentality of municipal government, namely, a commission in the office of the mayor composed of leading citizens charged with the responsibility of doing what they could to promote better intergroup relations within the community.*

In this vein Maryland, which had instituted an Interracial Commission in 1927, renamed it in 1943 the Commission to Study Problems Affecting the Colored Population. In Detroit the Mayor's Interracial Committee was founded in late 1943, the same year Los Angeles set up a Joint Committee for Interracial Progress, Chicago started its Mayor's Committee on Race Relations, and St. Louis began a Race Relations Commission. New York City set up the Mayor's Committee on Unity and Seattle started its Civic Unity Committee in 1944, while the Philadelphia Commission on Human Relations was founded in 1951. Spurred by the rise of racial tensions during the Second World War, by 1950 there were fifty-two municipal "intergroup relations" committees operating in seventeen states. In the words of one commentator, "Every week, it seemed, some new program of intercultural education, or interracial good-will, or another council on unity and amity appeared."

It is against this backdrop that the Cincinnati Mayor's Friendly Relations Committee (MFRC) was formed—not only as the local manifestation of a national trend, but more specifically in response to developments in Detroit.

In the summer of 1943 Cincinnati was worried. Earlier in the year, race rioting in Detroit had left thirty-four people dead, hundreds injured, and portions of the city in ashes. Racial tensions in Cincinnati were no different than in its smoldering counterpart to the north. Black women and men were engaged in the war effort as soldiers and defense workers, but most of Cincinnati's synagogues, churches, neighborhoods, and schools remained segregated, while discrimination was the norm in local government, labor unions, colleges, restaurants, swimming pools, skating rinks, hospitals, department stores, amusement parks, and movie theaters. Blacks in Cincinnati were just as frustrated with the racial status quo as their counterparts in Detroit.

Two months after the Detroit riot Arnold B. Walker, writing in the *Division of Negro Welfare Bulletin,* posed the question on everyone's mind: "Will There Be a Race Riot in Cincinnati?" Despite his acknowledgment of the prevailing racial tensions in the city, Walker concluded there would be no race riot in the city.

Nonetheless, the specter of Detroit loomed large in Cincinnati. Walker participated in a meeting with NAACP members and Mayor James G. Stewart just over two weeks after the Detroit riot to discuss ways to avoid similar turmoil in Cincinnati; the meeting was promoted under the heading This Must Not Happen Here. In the meeting it was agreed the mayor should convene a cross-section of citizens to form a "citizens committee on unity." On October 7, Stewart convened a group with representation from the Division of Negro Welfare, B'nai B'rith, the Council of Churches, the Public Recreation Commission, the Congress of Industrial Organizations, Catholic Charities, the Chamber of Commerce, and the black professional men in the Frontier Club with the aim of forming an intergroup relations committee sponsored by the city. On November 17 the Cincinnati City Council approved formation of the Mayor's Friendly Relations Committee (MFRC).

The city had a history of human relations initiatives before the immediate crisis of the Detroit riot, including those initiated by the Negro Civic Welfare Association (which later became the Greater Cincinnati Urban League) and the Woman's City Club of Greater Cincinnati (WCC). By 1927, for instance, the WCC had a race relations committee that actively promoted interracial understanding across the city, and in the early 1940s it founded the Fellowship House, an integrated organization dedicated to promoting interracial and ecumenical cooperation. Virginia Coffey, who would join the MFRC as assistant director in 1948, was an active participant in Fellowship House programs and was among the earliest black women admitted to membership in the Woman's City Club, in the late 1940s. Three presidents of the WCC would serve on the Mayor's Friendly Relations Committee, while others would serve on its successor, the Cincinnati Human Relations Commission. Although not directly rooted in the work of the WCC, these agencies would certainly be influenced by it. That influence apparently ran both ways because in the 1960s Coffey and her successor as assistant director at the MFRC, Eugene Sparrow, would be invited to speak at the WCC's civic luncheon on race and other human relations issues.

In addition to promoting racial peace and wartime cooperation, the MFRC was committed to a pluralistic vision of society in which all race and culture (if not class) groups were considered of equal value. Tolerance and a respect for differences were to be promoted over prejudice and discrimination. The committee planned to do this by means of education, persuasion, and persistent effort, a form of gradualism that did not involve protest, resistance, or public demonstrations. Thus the MFRC was designed from the outset to be a subtle behind-the-scenes

4

actor, an advisory body skilled in mediation but having no enforcement powers. The Cincinnati Mayor's Friendly Relations Committee was not unique but rather part of a national trend in setting up government-sponsored human relations organizations.

One hundred and nine citizens were appointed to the committee at its founding, of whom sixteen constituted a working Executive Committee. This unwieldy group initially led by its volunteer "secretary," Robert Segal of the Jewish Community Relations Council, met for lunch each month at the Ninth and Walnut Street YWCA "because that was the only place downtown that would serve blacks and whites together." The committee had no formal staff, operated with a $100 budget, and was thus often unable to respond effectively to the issues it was meant to address. But the group was able to organize and publish a newsletter, *Building Together*, and put on a luncheon honoring Paul Robeson, the athlete, actor, attorney, and activist.

The larger committee was broken down into subcommittees that "attacked such basic matters as employment, housing, schools, health, recreation, civil rights and police protection." But even in its early years the committee's efforts generated skepticism: "The more cynical and less progressive forces who become impatient often criticize this type of Citizen's Committee, saying they delay in tackling urgent problems." The skeptics may have had a point—"attacking" was a bit of hyperbole for the calm discussion, education, research, and persuasion that lay at the heart of the MFRC's agenda.

By 1944 the MFRC had organized a Friendly Relations Week (September 17–24), the highlight of which was a daylong Race Relations Institute featuring the executive secretary of the NAACP, Walter White. The committee's status began to improve after the city manager appropriated $10,000 for the MFRC's annual budget, and the committee opened an office in City Hall where Martha Ong acted as temporary executive director. With a budget in hand, the group set about looking for a permanent director.

Marshall Bragdon became the full-time executive director in 1945, a position he would hold for the next twenty years. In Bragdon's words, "a New York friend introduced me to Jeffrey Lazarus of Shillito's [now Macy's], who was hunting for an executive for Cincinnati's young Friendly Relations Committee. He rashly decided I might do; the Committee said OK; and I rashly accepted."

Born in Minneapolis, Bragdon attended Harvard as an undergraduate until forced to drop out by corrective surgery for the complications of polio he contracted in childhood. He went on to graduate from Wesleyan University, in Connecticut, and later became an editorial writer for the *Springfield (MA) Republican,* where he often wrote about reducing conflicts among social groups and the need to promote equality among all citizens. In addition to his work for the MFRC, Bragdon would become a founder and officer of the National Association of Intergroup Relations Officials and end his career as a consultant for the Community Relations Service of the U.S. Department of Justice.

The MFRC announced early on that it would not function as a black advocacy group. As Bragdon noted, "we are not working for the welfare of any one group, but are fostering improvements in conditions . . . which will safeguard the rights of all citizens." Nevertheless, its attention was almost entirely focused on race relations by the latter half of the 1940s.

In 1946, for example, four black men stopped a white couple and reportedly raped the woman while holding the man at gunpoint. Anger flared among white Cincinnatians, some of whom armed themselves, and mass meetings were called for. The MFRC tried to head off the specter of vigilantism and open violence by contacting religious and civic leaders to advise "common sense and moderation." This tense situation was eventually defused by the interventions of both black and white leaders. Subsequently the MFRC conducted a study that found that the local press and radio had added fuel to the racial fires by their "injudicious and even hysterical" reporting on the crime. Bragdon and an MFRC board member met with *Cincinnati Enquirer* editor Robert Ferger and *Cincinnati Times-Star* editor Hulbert Taft Sr., eliciting assurances that apparent racial conflicts would be reported with more restraint in the future.

Janet E. Smith, MFRC administrative assistant, in a summary of the agency's first five years, credited the committee with "the [resolution] of conflict and tension, thus preventing a riot in the summer of 1946. This single accomplishment alone may be said to justify the city's 'investment' in MFRC, for riots can cost a city untold sums in property damage, injury, loss of life, and repair of community relations." Clearly the MFRC did not single-handedly prevent a riot that summer, but Smith's comment shows how much the fear of rioting still resonated in Cincinnati three years after the Detroit upheaval.

Although it shared offices with the police division's race relations detail at city hall, the committee was frequently called upon to address issues of police harassment of black citizens. While the NAACP and other civic groups declared "war on police brutality," the MFRC continued to take a very understated and hands-off approach. This was the committee's stance in the 1946 case of Nathan Wright, a black ministerial student, who reported being abused and threatened by police. The police division and the city administration dismissed his accusations, inflaming the black community.

Caught in between, the MFRC decided to tread lightly, especially after city council member Gordon H. Scherer, foreshadowing the McCarthy era, suggested any criticism of the police was a Communist Party plot to "have the public lose confidence in the police departments as the opening wedge for overthrow of our government." In later public comments Marshall Bragdon acknowledged Communist critiques of American racism, but deflected Scherer's remarks by taking a human-relations tack: "the Communists can be answered only by millions of Americans taking up and living by the idea that the neighbor is to be respected and fairly treated, and what difference can be [sic] the color of his skin or his religion make, if he is a good man? By such behavior among Americans the Communists will be disarmed."

In the following year Haney Bradley, a black man, was severely beaten by police. A local judge dismissed disorderly conduct charges against Bradley, commenting that he saw no reason for the beating the defendant had received. Nonetheless, the city's safety director found no cause for disciplining the officers. In response, the Council of Churches, the NAACP, the Woman's City Club, the Jewish Community Council, and the West End Civic League sent a letter to city council criticizing police procedures and the safety director for ignoring "social attitudes and tensions in the community." The MFRC, although invited to be a signatory to the letter, declined to sign it. In both the Wright and the Bradley cases the committee, in keeping with its nonconfrontational, "impartial" stance, remained on the sidelines.

The committee's stated purpose of "promoting tolerance" instead of "taking sides" also affected its actions in the area of expanding employment opportunities as a means of improving relations "among races, among religious groups, and between labor and management." The committee adopted the stratagem of identifying employers who had integrated their workforces and proposing them as models for other companies to follow. When the West End Civic League took the more forceful position of picketing and leafleting employers resistant to integrating their workforces, the MFRC was called in as a mediator. The committee, represented by Bragdon, was marginally successful in this effort, which resulted in the hiring of two black workers and the publication of a pamphlet entitled *They Do Work Together.*

The MFRC continued its campaign to end discrimination in employment primarily through educational programs. As noted, it instituted its annual Friendly Relations Week in 1944, ever careful to indicate that this initiative included, but went well beyond, race relations. In 1948 the committee sponsored the local stop of the national Freedom Train, a mobile exhibition of famous documents from American history. This may have been one of the last echoes of the wartime civic unity movement; although the MFRC's immediate interest was in promoting equality and tolerance, it apparently saw a larger role in encouraging civic unity as well.

During this time, critics saw the MFRC as either duplicative of the efforts of other organizations (e.g., NAACP, the city's Negro Civic Welfare Association), ineffective in achieving its goals, or both. Despite attacks on the MFRC as a needless "frill" in the city budget, the city manager allocated $12,000 for the committee beginning in 1946. In 1948 two city council members balked at adding $1,000 to the MFRC's budget for staff cost-of-living increases. The raises for Marshall Bragdon and Janet Smith rankled AFL business manager Bernie Schmidt, who wanted equal treatment for all city hall employees who were members of his union. This issue brought on the committee's first administrative crisis and reorganization.

Caught between the union and the MFRC, city council compromised by offering to pay the committee a $15,000 lump sum to purchase its services on a contractual basis, provided the MFRC would become an independent, nonprofit organization. Despite misgivings by some MFRC board members that the agency would lose its official standing within the city, the committee incorporated as a nonprofit organization in early 1949. Marshall Bragdon noted publicly that it was still the mayor's committee because the mayor would continue to appoint its members and that little fundamental change in the activities or role of the committee would result from its new status.

In addition to its usual advising, promoting, cooperating, educating, and publishing roles, however, the newly independent MFRC was charged under its new articles of incorporation to "receive and investigate complaints and initiate its own investigations . . . of (a) racial, religious, and ethnic group prejudice, tensions, discrimination and disorder caused thereby; (b) practices of discrimination against any person because of race, color, creed, racial origin or ancestry." These investigations could result in nonbinding mediation or, more typically, in a report being issued. Moreover, the committee's funding would now come from contracts with "the City of Cincinnati or other organizations," a critical clause that would be used by both MFRC and later the CHRC to deflect charges in the 1950s and again in the 1970s of misuse of funds by the state auditor's office.

Throughout the late 1940s the committee continued its efforts to end segregation in the Cincinnati Bar Association, the Coney Island amusement park, local movie theaters, restaurants, roller- and ice-skating rinks, and bowling alleys, as well as the physician staffs of local hospitals. It opened a borrowing library of over one thousand books, pamphlets, and other literature on intergroup relations. The MFRC also worked with the public library, local radio stations, public school teachers, and the Girl Scouts to promote intergroup tolerance and co-operation. During this time the committee helped the conversion of the Council of Social Agencies' Division of Negro Welfare into the Cincinnati affiliate of the Urban League by donating $1,500 in discretionary monies for the new National Urban League office.

A signal event occurred in 1948, when Virginia Coffey, a native of West Virginia raised in Grand Rapids, Michigan, was hired as assistant director. Before joining the MFRC staff she taught in Cincinnati at the Harriet Beecher Stowe School, worked as an executive director of the West End YWCA branch, and formed the city's first African American Girl Scout troop. Upon arriving at the MFRC she set about writing a column for various newspapers titled Speaking Out on Race Relations and giving human relations talks to civic and religious groups, social clubs, business organizations, and PTAs. With added staffing, the committee was also able to begin reorganizing its voluntary committee and membership structures, which had fallen into disarray.

While the MFRC was being organized, in autumn of 1943, a group of "Negro Organizations Interested in Racial Amity and Good City

Government" sent a memo to Mayor Stewart and those active in the committee's formation. The group wanted the new committee to focus on inequities in "such basic problem [areas] as housing, health and welfare, employment, recreation, etc." These were considered the key underlying problems faced by blacks, of which rioting was only a symptom. The memo writers went on to note, "Whatever action is assumed by this committee, it should be clearly understood and publicized, *we do not regard ourselves as a committee to ward off race riots*. We do not expect rioting in Cincinnati" (emphasis in original). Nevertheless, Marshall Bragdon saw the Detroit riot and the tensions arising from the 1946 rape incident in Cincinnati as danger signs. In his words, "A riot-preventative was the first idea of the MFRC's role . . . we turned the corner safely [in 1946]. But a flare-up was too close for comfort." This is why he thought it prudent to establish an "emergency committee to act in [the] event of race riots" in 1949 in the wake of rioting in St. Louis when that city decided to integrate its oldest and largest swimming pool. The "Negro Organizations" that wrote the memo were prescient on two counts: no riots would occur in Cincinnati for another eighteen years, but the underlying problems of racial discrimination in housing, health and welfare, employment, and recreation, to name a few, would only continue to fester.

An informal evaluation of the MFRC's first five years shows little progress made in civil rights, police-community relations, and countering anti-Semitism, or in integrating employment, housing, health care, and recreational facilities. Nevertheless, Janet E. Smith ended her summary of the committee's first five years of activities with this insightful observation:

> Progress in human relations cannot be charted precisely; nor can the causes—the reasons for a success—be measured. All we can say is, the existence and the work of the MFRC has been helping the community to reduce discrimination and increase positive understanding between groups. This five-year history gives abundant evidence of such help, even though we cannot always estimate MFRC's exact contribution in each case.

The MFRC ended the 1940s true to its subtle roles of research, education, mediation, and persuasion. The committee's passive efforts were not satisfactory to some, and other groups took a more aggressive stance; for instance, the Cincinnati Citizen's Committee for Human Rights, formed in 1945, successfully began "visiting" restaurants that discriminated against black patrons. Nevertheless, the MFRC's policy of gradualism and discretion would enable it to continue its mission despite the chilling effects of early-1950s McCarthyism.

2

Intervening "in and between Crises"

The 1950s

The 1950s saw important progress toward desegregation at the national level. In Henderson v. United States, *the Supreme Court ruled that segregated seating on railroad dining cars denied the equal access to public accommodations guaranteed by the Interstate Commerce Act. In* Brown v. Board of Education of Topeka, *the court ruled that public school segregation violated the equal protection clause of the Fourteenth Amendment. In* McLaurin v. Oklahoma State Regents, *the court went on to rule that a public institution of higher learning could not treat a student differently because of his or her race. Accompanied by white protests and riots, the University of Alabama became integrated, as did Little Rock Central High School despite interference from Arkansas's Governor Orval Faubus. The organizational foundation for the Southern Christian Leadership Conference was laid in Atlanta. In 1957 the* Cincinnati Enquirer *published a four-part series on Appalachian migrants in the city; the lead article for the series shared the front page with another article headlined "Civil Rights Pact Is Proposed."*

Even with these signs of progress, however, racial atrocities were still being committed: Emmett Till, a fourteen-year-old African American youth visiting from Chicago, was beaten then shot to death in Tallahatchie County, Mississippi; the two white men charged with his murder were acquitted. Four years later Mack Charles Parker, an African American man accused of raping a white woman, was taken from jail by a mob in Poplarville, Mississippi, and lynched.

Marshall Bragdon opened the decade by reaffirming the MFRC's philosophy of how to achieve social change in remarks at its sixth annual meeting: "We must think of the prejudiced person as one needing help and education. Also, we realize that most discriminatory customs and arrangements will yield only to gradual but energetic treatment."

The committee's prestige would grow throughout the 1950s. Its 1949 annual meeting was attended by about a hundred people, and local news reporters noted those present included no representatives of the judiciary or the police division, only one city council member, a cameo appearance by the mayor, and very few blacks. Notably absent were representatives of the University of Cincinnati, where "the university band was all white, the College of Medicine had not admitted a Negro student in ten years, [and] the school still schedules games with Southern institutions which won't permit U.C. Negro athletes to play." But attendance at the 1952 annual meeting grew to 270, and by 1954 the MFRC celebrated its tenth anniversary by sending out seventeen hundred invitations eliciting attendance by delegates from 175 different organizations. The 1956 breakout sessions, which were a long-standing feature of the MFRC's annual meetings, featured seminars on civil rights, housing, churches, education, recreation, and Southern migrants.

In 1951, Dorothy N. Dolbey, a committee member since 1949, became the first woman to serve as chair of the MFRC, but her service ended after eight months when she resigned to become a Charter Committee candidate for city council. She would go on in the mid-1950s to serve as both vice-mayor and as acting mayor after the death of Mayor Edward Waldvogel. Dolbey was among several Cincinnatians who would use the MFRC and later the CHRC as a platform from which to launch a political career.

Meanwhile the three-person MFRC staff (Marshall Bragdon, Virginia Coffey, and Janet Smith) continued to address racial tensions in neighborhoods, parks, schools, and businesses from the twenty-by-twenty-foot confines of room 105 in City Hall. In this constricted space they met with various committee members, politicians, city administration officials, and citizens with complaints. Even after renovations increased the committee's office space, the city budget did not allow for additional furniture, so Marshall Bragdon spent several weekends purchasing materials out of his own pocket and building desks for the staff.

Despite space and financial constraints, the MFRC quietly went about its business with the close cooperation of city council member Theodore M. Berry, who would go on to become the city's first African American mayor. During the 1950s the MFRC adopted a two-pronged approach, working to improve human relations in both the governmental and the private sectors.

On the governmental front the committee successfully argued for integrating the swimming pools operated by the Recreation Commission and by the Cincinnati Public Schools. The MFRC defused the "problems" some feared would come with the hiring of the first black meter reader in the water department. In 1955 the city's first black firefighter was hired after the committee pointed out that an ordinance forbidding "discrimination in the appointment, promotion and remuneration of city employees" had been on the books for nine years.

Police-community relations remained at the top of the committee's governmental agenda throughout the decade. The police shooting of an unarmed black youth in Walnut Hills and the wounding of another citizen by a ricocheting bullet resulted in angry protests, but the city manager cleared the officers involved of any wrongdoing. According to Marshall Bragdon, "the MFRC's report did not make a judgment on that; its emphasis was on the obvious need for better police-citizen interchange, in and between crises." Some progress was made in this area when Stanley R. Schrotel, formerly of the Race Relations Detail, was named chief of police, and invited Bragdon to lecture each new recruit class for the following six years. In 1957, Chief Schrotel's picture appeared on the front cover of *Life* magazine along with an article lauding his department as a "Model Police Force" for the nation.

An incident involving the arrest of women in the West End for disorderly conduct drew crowds of five hundred to a thousand people over a period of two days. Tensions abated after the MFRC helped set up a meeting among black and white stakeholders. But the committee, distracted by other issues, did not follow up on the potential for better police-community relations that resulted. In Bragdon's words, "We did not build solidly for the long pull."

The MFRC did step up its in-service training at the police academy, but to little avail. In 1956 a black fifteen-year-old "errant schoolboy" was fatally shot by two police officers after he attacked them with a crowbar. The NAACP took up his case but a grand jury and the police chief exonerated the officers. In 1958 fourteen-year-old Abe Savage Jr. was shot to death by police after joyriding in his father's car and ignoring three roadblocks. Murder warrants filed by Abe Savage Sr. were dismissed, and the county prosecutor refused to take the case against the officers involved to a grand jury.

The MFRC undertook a study of these and several previous fatal shootings of black citizens by the police. The committee's findings were made public in a report stating that (1) there was no evidence of racial discrimination on the part of the police; (2) police officers were generally exercising good judgment; and (3) police procedures, training, and supervision were adequate. Marshall Bragdon summed up the committee's stance: "Evaluating the whole Abe Savage controversy, we have no doubt that it brought upon MFRC and its director sharp criticism and hostility from some quarters, and approbation from others . . . errors [were] made, but the community was somewhat better equipped to deal with the next contention."

Work in the schools continued apace throughout the decade. Most notable was Assistant Director Virginia Coffey's efforts to "raise the sights" of black students by recounting "Negro success stories." She visited schools across the city on this mission, at the same time working with Assistant Superintendent Wendell Pierce to identify and encourage black teachers to seek promotion to administrative posts.

Coffey's repertoire of success stories grew to include an X-ray technician, a city engineer, a beautician, a fireman, and an architect, to name a few. At Bloom Junior High students put on a play posing student actors as prospective dropouts encouraged to stay in school by other black students portraying adults who had stayed in school and "made it." At the play's end the real-life counterparts of the "successful adults" played by the students walked on stage and told their stories. In

Bragdon's words, "their presence and remarks were a hit, making 'opportunity' seem a bit more than a word." Bolstering Coffey's emphasis on the need to work with young people, in 1957 city council set up the Citizens' Committee on Youth, a sister agency contracting with the city alongside the MFRC.

Bragdon summarized the MFRC's passive role in governmental relations by noting that it functions "(1) as a consultant to government, in which role its advice is sought and participation welcomed in dealing with delicate, confidential matters; (2) as interpreter for disprivileged [*sic*] people needing a spokesman; (3) as a within-the-family critic, spotting errors, warning of consequences."

In the private sector the MFRC's objections to mounting minstrel shows at local high schools were heeded. Collaboration between the MFRC and the Cincinnati Committee on Human Relations, founded in the late 1940s, resulted in the acceptance of black students in both the Cincinnati Conservatory of Music and the College of Music of Cincinnati (which would later coalesce into the University of Cincinnati's College Conservatory of Music). A five-year "consultation" led by Virginia Coffey ended with the full integration of the local Girl Scout summer camping experience.

The MFRC was less successful, however, in urging the desegregation of Coney Island, an initiative complicated by the fact that only part of the 365-acre amusement park was within the city's jurisdiction. Opening the park to black patrons came piecemeal throughout the decade, culminating in full desegregation in 1961, primarily through the efforts of the Urban League and the NAACP. Also unresolved was the MFRC's objection to a union's using racial prejudice to force a restaurant to unionize its employees by "sending its Negro members to eat there in sudden numbers," thereby discouraging white patrons. The MFRC condemned this practice as a "cheap exploitation of racial prejudice," but only evoked a sharp rebuke from the union's attorney.

Another major endeavor of the MFRC during the 1950s was encouraging fair employment practices. Urged by city council member Berry, the MFRC joined a committee including the NAACP, the Urban League, the Jewish Community Relations Council, the Jewish Vocational Service, and the Ohio State Employment Service (OSES), to sponsor a study of the status of black participation in the workforce and black median incomes relative to those of whites. Using the 1950 census and other data sources, the research showed "median Negro family income in 1949 was 49% lower than the median white" and that "of job orders handled by OSES in a 10-week period, 76% specified 'white only.'"

Based on this information and the fact that the state legislature had repeatedly failed to adopt a Fair Employment Practices (FEP) bill, the MFRC issued its own report calling for a city ordinance "forbidding the practice of discrimination in employment against persons solely because of race, color, religious creed, national origin or ancestry by employers, employment agencies, labor organizations, and others." In 1953 the report was distributed citywide to citizens, pastors, and educators, as well as governmental and social service agency personnel.

This passive distribution of the fair employment report was unsatisfactory to some. Marian Spencer, a civil rights leader and early member of the MFRC, recalls,

I felt this was an excellent report and I lobbied strongly to have the report well publicized. I proposed a speaker's bureau and public meetings to discuss the report. Mr. Bragdon, the chair [*sic*], told me, "You don't know what we're about at the Mayor's Friendly Relations Committee." I said, "Oh yes I do, but the committee isn't doing it." I resigned.

The city council took four years to bring the MFRC's proposed ordinance to the floor, failing to pass it by a single vote. Three more years would go by until "in 1959 an Ohio Civil Rights Law was passed, much more effective than a city ordinance, which could not touch suburban discrimination." Richard Guggenheim, a member of the MFRC's board, was appointed chair of the new Ohio Civil Rights Commission. Bragdon credited the years of research and public education it took to get a statewide FEP law on the books with a modest "The whole effort was worth doing."

The MFRC had more tangible results in convincing Cincinnati's Civil Service Commission to delete the question "Are you white? Colored?" from its application forms. In cooperation with the Urban League, the NAACP, and the Jewish Community Relations Council, the MFRC convinced the Commission to record racial information after employment was secured, thus preventing a priori discrimination while allowing valuable data on employment opportunities for blacks to be collated and analyzed after the fact.

Ancillary to its efforts to promote fair employment practices was the committee's unsuccessful involvement in open-housing issues throughout the 1950s. It fought blockbusting practices in Avondale, where, despite meetings with white residents and the distribution of Not for Sale signs, white flight continued unabated. When the developers of Forest Park came to city council to contract for its water supply, a member of the council suggested including an open-housing requirement in the contract. The MFRC saw it as a "harsh dilemma" but stood quietly by as council approved a contract without an open-housing stipulation. Eleven years would pass before the suburb became racially integrated. In Evanston, Montgomery Road was considered the dividing line between black (west side) and white (east side) housing. After a black family bought a home two blocks east of Montgomery Road tensions in the neighborhood rose. According to Bragdon, "despite MFRC's and others' efforts to 'contage' calmness, the turnover was swift and frictional." The MFRC failed to convince the Kirby Road neighborhood to allow an integrated housing project proposed by the Cincinnati Metropolitan Housing Authority. Controversy over the project caused the CMHA to sell the tract to a private developer and the development remained all-white for the following ten years.

In keeping with its inclusive policy of improving understanding of all groups in the city, the committee turned its attention to the large numbers of white Southerners that began migrating to Cincinnati during and after the Second World War. In 1954 the MFRC sponsored a "Workshop on the Southern Mountaineer," led by Dr. Roscoe Giffin from Berea College. The committee subsequently developed a fifty-page written report that went to four printings and was used nationwide as a template for understanding the migrants' needs and concerns. A flurry of activity occurred in the ensuing years, including surveys of Appalachian migrants, sending representatives to the annual meetings of the Council of the Southern Mountains, and follow-up workshops aimed at "explaining" the migrants to educators and medical and social service providers.

Based on the MFRC's lead, similar workshops were organized in other cities as well. For instance, the Welfare Council of Metropolitan Chicago in cooperation with the Migration Services Committee of the Chicago Commission on Human Relations and the Mayor's Committee on New Residents held an Institute on Cultural Patterns of Newcomers in October of 1957. Four sessions were held "dealing with the four major immigrant groups in Chicago: the Southern Negro, the Southern Mountain White, the Puerto Rican, and the Mexican."

Nominations to the MFRC and its board were made by the committee itself and forwarded to the mayor, who made the appointments. Although the years between 1955 and 1960 marked the peak of Appalachian migration to the city, the MFRC never nominated an Appalachian representative to serve on the board or the committee at large. The racial turmoil of the 1960s would distract the committee from this constituency, but a reconstituted Cincinnati Human Relations Commission would return to an Appalachian focus in the 1970s.

In the late 1950s the MFRC also tried to get involved with the "several hundred" American Indians that were transferred from reservations to Cincinnati by the federal Urban Indian Relocation Program. The local Indian relocation office closed after the majority of the migrants left the city when their $80-a-week family stipend lapsed after four weeks, but those remaining were in dire straits. The relocation office refused to share names and addresses with the MFRC, but members of the Society of Friends, using local networks to find the remaining migrants, stepped in to offer assistance.

By mid-decade the MFRC's budget had risen to $21,130 and its staff had grown to four with the addition of a student intern, Paul. E. Ertle Jr. But by 1957, Bragdon was sounding a cautionary note based on the displacement caused by the construction of Interstate 75 in the West End, and on the school integration controversies in Arkansas and Alabama: "In Cincinnati there had been evidence and signs even 'before Faubus' of somewhat more intergroup anxiety and hostility. Such factors as the Southern conflict since 1954 and the local housing situation, urban renewal and neighborhood changes—these have probably overtaxed the city's existing means of helping Cincinnatians to adjust in new conditions."

Reflecting on the work of the MFRC during the decade of the 1950s, Marshall Bragdon noted, "what MFRC did seems now rather ineffectual, against the magnitude of the problems. In review we see where more or different or earlier action should have been attempted." The challenges and achievements of the 1960s were about to begin, and growing racial antagonism, what Bragdon called "the northward ricochet of southern conflict," was about to hit Cincinnati and the MFRC.

3

Working with "Social Dynamite"

The 1960s

During the 1960s racial tensions grew more heated nationwide even as the civil rights movement became more powerful. President John F. Kennedy issued two executive orders, one establishing the President's Committee on Equal Employment Opportunity to investigate racial discrimination by government contractors, and another requiring fair housing practices across all federal programs involved in real estate transactions. More than two hundred thousand people attended the March on Washington for Jobs and Freedom, where Martin Luther King Jr. delivered his "I Have a Dream" speech. The Civil Rights Act was passed, strengthening federal power to protect voting rights; prohibiting discrimination in public accommodations; authorizing the attorney general to file suits for the desegregation of schools and public facilities; barring discrimination in federally assisted programs; prohibiting discrimination by employers and unions; and creating an Equal Employment Opportunity Commission with investigative and mediation powers. Voting Rights and Fair Housing Acts were also passed. President Lyndon B. Johnson issued an executive order requiring all federal contractors and subcontractors to take "affirmative action" to hire and promote persons without regard to race. Johnson went on to appoint Thurgood Marshall the first African American justice on the Supreme Court.

But this progress was bittersweet: leaders Medgar Evers and Martin Luther King were assassinated. Four black girls were killed in a church bombing in Alabama and three civil rights workers were murdered in Mississippi, their bodies buried under an earthen dam. Rioting killed hundreds of others in major cities across the country.

In Cincinnati, the decade started off with the police killing of two brothers, Charles and Virgil Brady. Police Chief Schrotel found the shootings justified, while the NAACP called the police action against the black youth "an unwarranted use of force under the circumstances" and requested that city council consider the possibility of instituting a police review board. A long and contentious public hearing seven months after the shootings resulted in the decision that, in light of the Brady case, instituting a review board would be "profitless." The MFRC neither supported nor opposed the review board proposal, simply saying it "merited more study," and continued its police-community relations policy of consulting, studying, and training.

When the Cincinnati NAACP picketed local Woolworth stores for the chain's refusal to serve black patrons in its cafeteria and for discriminatory hiring practices, the MFRC lauded the association's fight against economic and psychological discrimination. In a nod to the McCarthyism of the past decade, Marshall Bragdon went on to note that the NAACP "has also helped make the Communist wooing of American Negroes an utter flop."

The committee continued to argue against racial references in newspaper real estate ads, against the all-white composition of the Cincinnati Real Estate Board (finally integrated in 1964), and against neighborhoods closed to black home buyers. A proposed city ordinance, aimed at rectifying these problems and endorsed by the MFRC, failed to pass. In his speech at the 1962 annual meeting, Bragdon stated, "The biggest problem looming is the one catalogued 'race and housing.'" A *Cincinnati Post and Times-Star* editorial marking the twentieth anniversary of the MFRC, in 1963, suggested that while some doors to employment and recreation had been unlocked, major obstacles to equality remained: "The Negro can buy anything today in a free market but a house."

The MFRC's insistence on facts over rumors did help quell tensions in the school system, first over the painting of a swastika at Ach Junior High, then over several fights in and near local public schools. The former was determined to be juvenile vandalism rather than organized anti-Semitism, while the fights involving black and white students "had no definite racial origin." However, the hyperbolic reporting of these events in the media caused the MFRC to consult again with local news outlets with the result that, according to Bragdon, "the newsmen did their job more carefully thereafter."

The committee was prescient in recognizing the "social dynamite" of unemployed black youth in the nation's cities. It circulated fifteen hundred copies of a paper by Dr. James Conant identifying the hopelessness that came from "past deprivations, employment discrimination, and now a shrinkage of unskilled jobs." Despite the MFRC's warning and well-meaning attempts to ameliorate the situation, this explosive mixture in Cincinnati would ignite in just a few years.

In the early 1960s the MFRC gained prominence nationally by hosting the annual meeting of the National Association of Intergroup Relations Officials (NAIRO), and internationally by sending Virginia Coffey to England to consult on urban race relations issues. She visited seven British cities that were experiencing high levels of immigration from former colonies in Africa. In addition to helping the cities identify and ameliorate causes of racial strife, Coffey noted that she "placed high value on the supporting role of municipal government, and the teamwork of paid staff and citizen volunteers defusing tense racial situations." In short, she was promoting the MFRC model in England.

Coffey resigned after nearly fifteen years of staff service to the MFRC. Feeling isolated in the "Ivory Tower" of city hall, she told an interviewer, "we didn't really know what was happening and couldn't *feel* [emphasis in original] what was happening. . . . I had the conviction I wanted to get out there with the populace." She went to work for Seven Hills Neighborhood Houses and later Memorial Community Center in low-income black and Appalachian neighborhoods such as the East End, the West End, and Over-the-Rhine. Coffey was replaced by Eugene Sparrow, who was trained at the Harvard Divinity School and came to Cincinnati from the Springfield, Massachusetts, Urban League. Six years later Coffey would return to become the first woman to serve as executive director of the Cincinnati Human Relations Commission.

In the early 1960s the MFRC was becoming an ever more mar-
ginal actor. Antidiscrimination efforts led by the NAACP, CORE, the
Ohio Civil Rights Commission, and several Protestant churches over-
shadowed the more passive tactics of the MFRC. The fuse on the social
dynamite was burning while the agency held monthly potluck dinners
for board members, staff, and others "who needed to know more of the
parts and people of the city."

In 1963 the NAACP publicly questioned how the MFRC could help
control potentially explosive racial incidents "when the Negro community has very little regard for the MFRC." Outgoing MFRC board chair
Arthur Hull Jr. appointed a group to evaluate the committee's "format,
methods and adequacy to meet new demands," and launched a ten-
month self-study that concluded, "We recommend the establishment of
a new Human Relations Commission with the responsibilities, powers,
and sanctions heretofore described. The Commission would be a per-
manent and integral part of city government." Part of the rationale
given for the recommendation stated, "Negroes' new self-image, the rise
of non-violent direct action, and other ways of demanding equal opportunity now: these confront an unprepared white majority nurtured on a
diet of gradualism. All this can lead to sharp community tensions—or
be part of sound progress if heeded and guided wisely."

On November 22, 1963, a complete reevaluation of the city's human
relations efforts was submitted to city council for its consideration. Unfortunately, that was the same day President Kennedy was assassinated
and the report was "lost in the shuffle." Board chair S. Arthur Spiegel
and his successor, Robert L. Black Jr., were determined to modernize
human relations work in the city, but it would take two more years to get
approval for the MFRC's successor, the Cincinnati Human Relations
Commission.

In May 1964, Joseph Leinwohl, Hull's successor as chair of the
MFRC, introduced five of his commission colleagues to city council's
Welfare Committee, along with Richard Marks, executive of the Detroit Commission on Community Relations. This group, which included
Marshall Bragdon, presented basic arguments for forming a human
relations commission instead of reforming the MFRC, but what they
actually sought was an administrative rather than a functional change.
The MFRC, operating under a purchase-of-services contract was considered a "quasi-governmental" agency, and thus deemed "outmoded

by sweeping social change." The proposal sought a name change to the Cincinnati Human Relations Commission, full integration with city government so the commission could claim the "*prestige* of an official City agency," (emphasis in original) and civil service status for the staff:

> A *revision* (not a drastic change) in the City's official involve-
> ment with human relations matters is clearly in order, a revision
> which will bring this vital function directly under the umbrella
> of City government and subject it to the attention and direction
> of the City.
>
> Basic functions of MFRC do not need either major additions
> or deletions. Objectives and general areas of activity of the exist-
> ing MFRC need merely to be strengthened and continued under
> the *direct* guiding eye of Council and City Administration . . .
>
> The proposed Human Relations Commission should be
> afforded the same dignity, authority, and general recognizance
> [*sic*] as other non-enforcement departments in city government.
> The professional staff members of the MFRC are dedicated
> high-caliber, and conscientious workers. They should have
> available to them the same pension, retirement, and other bene-
> fits which are available to City employees . . .
>
> Any organization charged with the responsibility of main-
> taining good relations in a major city especially at a time when
> there is more social turbulence than any time in that city's his-
> tory, should be more than a "contract" agency. The MFRC
> should be replaced with a Human Relations Commission
> which does not work on contract with the City, but is instead an
> established part of city government. (emphasis in original)

This proposal came under immediate attack from the business community, with some leaders charging that the former agency was, for instance, already duplicating the efforts of the police division in keeping
civic order, and of the Civil Service Commission in providing equal
employment opportunities in local government. Perhaps most telling
was the criticism that "the MFRC has been most ineffective, and all that
the CHRC will be is a dressed up MFRC."

On March 17, 1965, the Cincinnati city council passed an ordinance
providing for the establishment of the agency that would supplant the

MFRC, the Cincinnati Human Relations Commission. Key changes recommended by the commissioners were not included, however; the CHRC remained an independent contractor and its staff did not receive the benefits or protections of city hall employees. The name change was adopted, and the mayor and city council were substituted for the city manager's office under new reporting guidelines.

The new Cincinnati Human Relations Commission was also a somewhat streamlined version of the MFRC administratively, with eighteen voting members meeting monthly (versus thirty-six on the former committee) and a "general committee" of one hundred meeting monthly. Contrary to the recommendations of some on the committee, the CHRC received no new powers of subpoena or enforcement.

The new form of the CHRC met with some bureaucratic resistance. Reflecting on those days, Marshall Bragdon wrote, "in 1965 the city agreed to a new form of the agency . . . even at the cost of some abrasiveness. Possible sources of abrasion were some competition with the Civil Service Commission and some competition with private organizations fighting the same battles. Sensitivity was necessary to prevent the CHRC from stepping over into other people's areas."

Not much for sensitivity but a great one for clarity, new board chair S. Arthur Spiegel laid out the boundaries of the new commission's work in letters to the Civil Service Commission, and emphatically refuted public criticisms leveled against the CHRC by some businesspeople and members of the city administration.

The change to the CHRC also spelled the end of Marshall Bragdon's tenure as executive director. Spiegel, who oversaw the transition from the MFRC to the CHRC, commented: "I think, unfortunately, civil rights organizations like the NAACP, Congress of Racial Equality, the Council of Churches and others thought, possibly unfairly, that the time had swept by Marsh Bragdon and that he was not functioning as successfully as they would like." Bragdon tendered his resignation in April and the assistant director, Eugene Sparrow, was appointed acting director of the CHRC in July. A testimonial luncheon for Bragdon held at the Sheraton-Gibson Hotel in July featured speakers from the MFRC board and staff, the Cincinnati Police Division, the Ohio Civil Rights Commission, and NAIRO; notably absent from the dais were representatives of the NAACP, the Urban League, and CORE.

It was business as usual for the newly constituted CHRC: studying housing issues and advising neighborhoods about integration; encouraging the city to avoid discrimination in hiring, especially new police recruits; and instituting a new subcommittee focusing on urban Appalachians. The commission's biggest initiative, with the Building Trades Council, was fairly unproductive but illustrative.

A new convention center, seven new public schools, new buildings at the University of Cincinnati and at local hospitals were causing a construction boom across the city. Despite the craft unions' refusal to cooperate, a CHRC study found widespread discrimination against hiring black workers for these projects. CORE and the NAACP organized demonstrations and sit-ins at construction sites, while the CHRC sent its report to city council, which in turn forwarded it to the Ohio Civil Rights Commission. Frustrated by the bureaucratic maneuvering, the CHRC tried to organize a meeting among contractors and building trades leaders; thirty-eight contractors agreed to attend but the Building Trades Council refused, and the initiative fell apart.

In August 1966, Eugene Sparrow left Cincinnati to become the executive director of the Grand Rapids Human Relations Commission. Clinton L. Reynolds served as acting director from August through December of that year. David D. McPheeters, a University of Cincinnati graduate and former staff member of the Urban League of New York, became executive director of the CHRC on December 1. Under McPheeters the CHRC board was again slimmed down to "9 to 12" members because the board was having a difficult time achieving a quorum. It had a budget of slightly over $71,000 and a staff of "five inter-group relations specialists and two clerical aids." McPheeters found the agency fairly ineffective: "The CHRC cannot compel anyone to do anything. It operates outside the aegis of the city administration and is answerable to City Council on all matters of operation and policy. . . . As far as the so-called working relationship with the city administration is concerned, it is a spotty, insincere farce."

In terms of programs, the CHRC continued to urge school desegregation, published a three-years-in-the-making manual entitled *Human Relations in Housing*, and demoted urban Appalachians to mere "migrants" in a brief afterthought appended to its 1966 annual report. More significantly, the CHRC achieved some progress on the employment front by successfully urging a contract compliance plan for city government that included an equal-opportunity clause. The plan gave the CHRC responsibility for monitoring compliance and made a commission staff member the secretary of the Compliance Board.

The commission also helped launch Project JUMP (Journeyman Union Manpower Program) aimed at increasing the qualifications of black workers for both apprentice and journeyman positions in the unionized building trades. The Greater Cincinnati Vocational Foundation was created to receive $281,500 in funding from the U.S. Labor Department, while the CHRC was subcontracted to provide recruitment, counseling, and follow-up services for JUMP trainees. Unfortunately, the CHRC became involved in squabbles over money and control that caused great dissension both with the foundation and within the commission's board and staff. External events, however, were about to overshadow the internal dissension wracking the commission.

Within the first month of taking office McPheeters wrote an extensive report titled "A Proposed Plan to Prevent Riots," signaling the CHRC's fear of local unrest similar to the 1965 riot in Watts and more proximately the 1966 rioting in Cleveland's predominantly black Hough neighborhood. McPheeters felt Cincinnati was on the verge of a riot and said so at the annual meeting of the CHRC, a position that was not well received:

> the speech I made at the Netherland Plaza at our annual meeting was one that . . . stirred up a lot of trouble in Cincinnati. . . . when I got to the annual meeting they asked me what I thought of Cincinnati. I said that I think that Cincinnati is on the brink of being another victim of a Los Angeles type of riot, because I know what is going on in the minority community. And I'm not going to tell you a lie. I won't lie to the people I'm working with or for. I will not lie.

McPheeters's administratively complex and expensive plan called for both a Bi-Racial Commission to deal with governmental issues (legislative, judicial, executive) and a Civic Bi-Racial Committee to work with business, labor, religious, educational, social, and civic groups. The ink was barely dry on this elaborate plan before rioting erupted in Cincinnati.

Posteal Laskey Jr., a black man, was convicted in May 1967 for raping and murdering six white women. A family member was arrested in Cincinnati's Avondale neighborhood while publicly protesting Laskey's innocence and raising money for his defense. A mass protest at the corner of Rockdale Avenue and Reading Road on June 12 erupted into several days of violent unrest that spread through seven other neighborhoods. Seven hundred National Guard troops were sent to restore order; by June 15, an uneasy calm was reinstituted after one person was killed, sixty-three were injured, and 404 were arrested.

McPheeters was in Washington, DC, when the rioting broke out; the CHRC board felt he was slow in returning to the city to deal with the crisis, and he resigned under pressure on July 13, less than nine months after being appointed the CHRC's first executive director. In an interview McPheeters sheds a different light on his trip to Washington:

> I had to go out to Washington. We were running out of money [for Project JUMP] and I had to talk to people in the Labor Department. It was June the 13th in 1967. I went to Washington and before I was to see the people over at the Labor Department, I went over to Ted Berry's office because Ted worked for Sargent Shriver. He said, What are you doing in Washington? I'm here to go into the Labor Department to see about raising the funding for this JUMP program. He said, do you know what happened in Cincinnati last night? I said, no, what? He said they had a riot. You better get back there in a hurry because if you don't, you could be a scapegoat. I said, O my God. . . . It scared the daylights out of me. I couldn't get a plane out until the next day when I phoned for reservations; nothing to Cincinnati that I could get on. And when I got on and got back to Cincinnati, all of a sudden I was accosted by a lot of people asking me where was I when the riots broke out. . . . I was in Washington trying to bring money in. I never got the money. I came back as soon as I could. They tell me I was part of this riot. They thought that [I] got out of town because [I] didn't want to be seen as part of it.

Before leaving the commission McPheeters wrote another report giving his analysis of the riot. According to McPheeters, housing in Cincinnati's predominantly black West End was lost by the construction of Interstate 75, forcing many families into South Avondale, where real estate blockbusters carved formerly spacious housing into poorly maintained, high-density units. Crime and blight soon followed. City efforts at rehabilitation in the area mainly benefited the University of Cincinnati and nearby hospitals rather than neighborhood residents. Frustrations were already high in Avondale when the Laskey protests began.

The CHRC expressed frustration with McPheeters's report "because it offers little by way of constructive solution to the racial problems in Cincinnati" but went on to say it was "the authentic cry of a person who feels himself imprisoned and caught between conflicting factions." The report was not widely circulated, and a highly redacted version was sent to city council.

The rioting also cost police chief Jacob W. Schott Sr. his job. He resigned in 1967 but made national news by testifying before the U.S. Senate Judiciary Committee that there were no ghettos in Cincinnati, that black residents were evenly distributed among the police precincts, and that a handful of agitators including H. Rap Brown, Stokely Carmichael, and Martin Luther King were responsible for inciting the riots. Schott cast the issue as one of maintaining law and order in the face of chaos. The chair of the CHRC, Robert L. Black Jr., publicly refuted Schott's comments as "misleading and superficial" while pointing to the many sociological factors causing racial tension that had been clearly identified in various CHRC studies. Black framed the issue as one of people tired of inequity who were seeking justice.

The annual report summarizing the CHRC's status at the end of 1967 is telling. In addition to the "deterioration of the JUMP program" it notes,

> Post-riot activities were aimed at finding and suggesting ways and means of resolving basic conflicts and attitudes which underlie the polarization within the community. The Commission did its best to interpret what had happened in the community, and why. The Commission was depressed by the realization that what it recommended and what it had to say fell on deaf ears.
>
> The latter part of the year was devoted to what in other situations has been called "an agonizing reappraisal." This arose from the lack of any visible success from past programs,

continuing internal difficulties, the resignations of the Executive Director, the Assistant Director and other staff members, and the very apparent need to re-think and re-state the function and task of the Commission.

During part of 1967 the CHRC had no executive or deputy director, the staff was down to two professionals and a secretary, and the commission's only source of income, $69,000 from the city, was in jeopardy. The low ebb of the CHRC in 1967 resulted in rumors that the CHRC would be disbanded; Mayor Eugene Ruehlmann called the rumors "nonsense" but instituted changes in the commission's operating procedure that had the agency reporting through him to city council. In an early 1968 editorial the *Cincinnati Enquirer* stated:

> The Cincinnati Human Relations Commission is not yet two years old. . . . Yet the commission has scarcely known a week without controversy. . . . The fact of the matter, however, is that the commission has pleased practically no one.
> To say that Cincinnati doesn't need some agency working in the field of human relations is to say that problems simply don't exist. Everyone knows better. We hope that the effort to breathe a more useful life into the Human Relations Commission succeeds. Cincinnati has enough crusaders in the field; its need is for some quiet, effective persuaders.

Three turmoil-filled years after its inception, the CHRC would settle on an executive director who was both a crusader for human rights and a quiet, effective persuader.

The commission set up a selection committee "directed to fill the position of Executive Director and the new position of Deputy Director with the most experienced and qualified persons available." In February of 1968 Virginia Coffey returned to the CHRC as its new executive director; Thomas L. Garner was selected as her deputy. Garner, a graduate of Woodward High School and the University of Cincinnati, previously worked as neighborhood coordinator for the Better Housing League. Clinton L. Reynolds, who was assistant director under McPheeters and had served as interim director after his resignation, left the CHRC's staff following Coffey's appointment.

Virginia Coffey was executive director less than two months when racial tensions in Cincinnati again escalated following the assassination of Martin Luther King. An April 8 memorial service in Avondale attended by some fifteen hundred people was orderly until a black merchant trying to prevent his Avondale store from being robbed accidentally shot and killed his wife. Rumors circulated that his wife was killed by white police officers and the ensuing riot lasted until April 12. Despite a curfew and the presence of fifteen hundred National Guard troops, some seventy fires were set, two people were killed, many were injured, and 204 people were arrested.

Throughout this time, Virginia Coffey and Thomas Garner represented the CHRC both in city hall and among Avondale Community Council (ACC) members. After the King assassination, schools across the city began closing. According to an internal CHRC report, "the mayor was distressed and deplored the possibility of schools being dismissed and putting all of those children on the street who might get something started." On behalf of Mayor Ruehlmann Coffey phoned Paul Miller, superintendent of schools, requesting he not allow this to happen. Miller responded that it was the decision of individual principals who were already being faced with "unruly" students and others engaged in hallway sit-ins in honor of King. Coffey wondered aloud whether principals and staff "might not be ingenious enough to plan memorial programs for the day, with students doing the planning, performing, etc." Nevertheless the schools continued to close, putting students on the streets.

Coffey and Garner continued to mediate between the city, the Avondale Community Council, the West End Community Council, and unnamed "groups of militants." Their advice on behalf of the CHRC was sought by the mayor, various city council members, the safety director, police chief, city manager, city solicitor, and National Guard officers. When local clergy announced a Sympathy March in Avondale demonstrating their sorrow at Dr. King's death to coincide with a black-only memorial service for King, four representatives of the CHRC joined the effort to dissuade them. "The white clergymen were present and were made to understand, very emphatically, that their March would not be welcomed."

While clerical staff maintained the CHRC office on Black Monday, the day of the King memorial service in Avondale, other staff and board members were in the West End, Mt. Auburn, Walnut Hills, and Avondale monitoring conditions in each neighborhood. Thomas Garner attended a briefing for black police officers assigned to the memorial service. Virginia Coffey met at the office of the Avondale Community Council with two black CHRC board members and attended the memorial service with them. She was very complimentary of the ACC's security guards, citizens who tried to maintain order by directing traffic, helping disperse the crowd, and protecting neighborhood businesses. But their efforts were in vain after the accidental shooting at the Avondale store, which occurred just after the memorial service concluded:

> Shortly afterward, [ACC officer] Clyde Vinegar took Mrs. Coffey by the hand, approached [police] Specialist Hill, and indicated he should call in the police stationed just outside of the area; that things had gotten out of hand, and people could no longer be controlled. Specialist Hill made the call and Mrs. Coffey and Tom Garner left. As they left heavy billows of smoke were coming from [the intersection of] Rockdale [Avenue] and Reading Road and people were moving from the area fast.

CHRC staff and board members did what they could to intervene in a tense situation over which they had no control. An internal memo, while not completely objective, summarized the CHRC's activities in the tumultuous times of April 1968 in glowing terms:

> The CHRC's involvement was significant and timely. Board and staff assisted city officials in arranging communication between them and community leaders; served as a consultant to the Mayor, school superintendent and others. Also were active participants in Negro community program[s]; issued statements to press when necessary; received complaints. In so doing, confidence in the agency is growing and a positive image is being achieved.

In the closing months of the decade Coffey turned her attention to reorganizing the commission into five divisions: Community Relations, Education, Employment, Land Use, and Law. Within each division there were from three to seven committees tasked with (1) "advising and consulting" (e.g., with unions and contractors on hiring practices); (2) "participating" (e.g., studies, research, publications); (3) "training" (e.g., public speaking, sensitivity training for police and firefighters); and (4) "observing" (e.g., sending representatives to meetings of the school board or the community chest). Coffey also asked for additional staff to implement this new structure, particularly "field workers," who would focus on the West End, Over-the-Rhine, Mt. Auburn, Avondale, Walnut Hills, and Evanston.

4

Moving from Stability

to "Complete Disarray"

The 1970s

Early in the decade the Supreme Court upheld a court-ordered busing plan designed to achieve racial balance in North Carolina's Charlotte-Mecklenburg school system. The case, brought by the NAACP, set a nationwide precedent. A year later Congress passed the Equal Employment Opportunity Act of 1972, giving the Equal Employment Opportunity Commission the power to file class-action lawsuits and extending its jurisdiction to cover state and local governments as well as educational institutions. However, the Supreme Court ruled against universities using fixed racial quotas in making admissions decisions, a challenge to affirmative action.

Locally, the U.S. District Court for the Southern District of Ohio found that Cincinnati realtors were engaging in racial steering. The plaintiffs, including the Coalition of Neighborhoods, sought a declaration of their rights under federal law and an injunction against future racial steering by the defendants. The parties eventually entered into a settlement agreement, which provided that the realtors would not engage in racial steering. Seven Cincinnati police officers would be killed in the line of duty during the 1970s, leading to the appointment of the Hawkins Commission and the establishment of the city's Office of Municipal Investigations.

U nder Virginia Coffey's direction the CHRC board was expanded to its former complement of eighteen and the staff grew to over twenty. The CHRC board and staff worked with local and state officials to have Martin Luther King's birthday declared a legal holiday. The training of police and fire recruits continued apace even as the commission processed citizens' complaints of police mistreatment. The majority of other complaints investigated were from city workers dissatisfied with their treatment on the job, and parents of students concerned about racial incidents in the public schools.

As early as 1971, Coffey identified good police-community relations as "the most pressing need in every urban center in the country." The plan she devised foreshadowed the nationally recognized Cincinnati Police-Community Relations Collaborative, an agreement entered into in 2002:

> [CHRC field staff would arrange] conferences or meetings between citizens and city officials to deal with racial matters having tension and conflict potential. The abrasive relationship between the police and minority communities is a major and explosive source of grievance and tension. Field staff must do everything possible to bridge the gap between neighborhood people and police. This can be done by organizing and staffing small intimate meetings between police on the beat and grass roots people.

Relations with the police division improved slightly with the appointment of Carl Goodin as chief; the CHRC staff and board members began nighttime "ride alongs" with officers on patrol. Overall police-community relations remained poor, however, despite monthly meetings between the CHRC's law division and Chief Goodin. During an incident in Over-the-Rhine in 1972, police arrested James Harris, a black CHRC field-worker. He was encouraging several dozen black and white youths who had gathered for a fight to obey police orders to disburse. Harris explained to officers on the scene he was trying "to prevent a bad situation," but he was ignored and arrested for illegally blocking the sidewalk. The police later claimed Harris never tried to identify himself, even though he was wearing a red coat with Cincinnati Human Relations Commission written on the back in two-inch letters. In a complaint lodged with the city manager, Thomas Garner, the CHRC's deputy director, maintained that "the police report on the incident was completely false." Subsequent meetings attempted to "clarify policies" governing the interactions of police officers and CHRC staffers attempting to intervene in street-level altercations.

One of Coffey's efforts as executive director was to reinvigorate the organization's waning attention to the Appalachian community. Aware of Marshall Bragdon's efforts in this regard over the two previous decades, she converted his top-down social-service approach into a grass-roots empowerment strategy.

For example, nearly ten years after the inaugural conference on Southern migrants, the MFRC under Bragdon had sponsored another conference in 1963. All the "right" people were there—the health commissioner, the superintendent of schools, the welfare director, along with representatives of the municipal court, the city housing division, and the state office of employment services, to name a few—and discussing the "poor adjustments" made by the newcomers. Although folks from the Council of the Southern Mountains and Berea College also got a word in, invited participation from the local Appalachian community was minimal. Urban Appalachians were considered the topic, not the experts.

Virginia Coffey had a different perspective gained from her years as a staff person at the Riverview Neighborhood House in the East End and as director of Memorial Community Center in Over-the-Rhine. In both places she worked closely with Appalachian neighborhood leaders, coming to respect their ability to meet the challenges they were encountering.

True to her vision of the CHRC helping to empower all groups in the city, Coffey led the effort to help establish the Urban Appalachian Council (UAC). In 1971 with the CHRC's endorsement, the week of April 17–21 was declared Appalachian Week in the city, the Junior League of Cincinnati held the first Appalachian Festival at Music Hall, and "Appalachians in an Urban Environment" was the topic of an all-day conference held in conjunction with the festival.

Despite opposition from some members of the commission, Coffey worked closely with Appalachian leaders Ernie Mynatt and Michael Maloney, initially through the Appalachian Committee, later hiring Maloney to be the "Appalachian specialist" on her staff, and finally providing partial funding to help the Appalachian advocacy organization establish a CHRC field office while it gained the momentum to become a freestanding agency in 1974. It was at this time that the CHRC sponsored a report by Maloney called "The Social Areas of Cincinnati: An Analysis of Social Needs." Decennial updates of this census-based study, which included black and Appalachian neighborhoods, would continue to inform social-service decision making in the city for the next fifty years.

Coffey's vision of the CHRC as an incubator for self-governing advocacy organizations such as the UAC would, in subsequent decades, lead the commission to support the rights of ex-felons, the LGBTQ community, people with physical or mental disabilities, coalitions of neighborhoods, and others. Virginia Coffey was sixty-four when she took on the role of executive director and was approaching seventy when she left the post in December 1973, noting, "Most people leave positions when things are in turmoil, but I decided that things are in such good shape that I could bow out now without causing any upset."

According to Arzell Nelson, whom she mentored at the CHRC, it was not an easy departure, "Mrs. Coffey had a tough time in her later years. To be honest with you, the real secret is that she was really forced out of the CHRC. Yeah. It was sad because she didn't have enough retirement [savings]. . . . They forced her out of the CHRC because they said she was too old and it was time for her to go."

Adding to the unease of her departure, Ohio state auditor Thomas E. Ferguson challenged a $2,191 retirement payment the CHRC board made to her (based on one week's salary for each four years of her employment as well as for accumulated vacation pay) and demanded she return those funds. This was old hat for the agency because in the mid-1950s then state auditor James Rhodes challenged the entire appropriation city council made to the MFRC as illegal. Marshall Bragdon quietly but firmly pointed out that the auditor was wrong because his challenge was based on the out-of-date 1943 resolution founding the MFRC rather than the contract for services the city had entered into with the committee in 1949.

In similar fashion, the CHRC board, which included several attorneys, fired back a three-page letter pointing out to Ferguson that the board had scrupulously followed its own articles of incorporation; moreover, the State of Ohio had no jurisdiction over the internal workings of a private corporation such as the CHRC. The letter chastised the auditor for "cast[ing] a shadow on the integrity of Mrs. Virginia Coffey" and officially requested "a public apology to Mrs. Coffey and the CHRC." There is no record of either an apology from Ferguson or a refund from Coffey.

Ethelrie Harper was a staff representative of District 51 of the American Federation of State, County, and Municipal Employees, and served on the CHRC board from 1971 until her death, in 1975. A native of Meridian, Mississippi, Harper was a widely respected community and civic leader. To honor her work for the CHRC as well as in the civil rights and labor movements, the commission established the Ethelrie Harper Humanitarian Award, which has been given annually since 1976.

After serving as deputy director, Thomas Garner began his eight-year tenure as the CHRC's executive director in 1974. A former captain in the U.S. Air Force, Garner would need all his tactical skills to navigate the turbulence the CHRC was about to encounter.

The latter half of the 1970s was one of constant turmoil for the CHRC. City council members were concerned with dissention within the commission and "put commission members on notice to 'get their act together' or risk losing their contract." Council member and former CHRC staff member J. Kenneth Blackwell noted the city had no power to disband the agency, but without a city contract it would become "an independent, nonprofit agency without a client." The city council discussed cutting $72,000 from the CHRC budget (roughly a quarter of that year's allocation) and "eliminating housing and education projects from CHRC's duties."

Throughout 1977 the commission was riven by multiple internal fights leading to four board resignations and a threat to Garner's position as executive director. The *Cincinnati Enquirer* noted the resignations came among "charges, counter-charges, and outright name calling among some of the city's 'experts' on handling sensitive issues." The protracted disputes appeared to involve personalities as much as issues and left the CHRC in "complete disarray."

The internal and external clashes continued throughout 1978 and 1979, years when the CHRC was deeply at odds with the city manager, various city council members, the police division, and even itself. Examples include:

- The city council lost patience when, two years after its request for a fair marketing plan for housing was made to the CHRC, nothing had been produced; the council subsequently opted to switch a contract for promoting fair housing from the commission to Housing Opportunities Made Equal.

- The CHRC's effort to promulgate an unwieldy human relations ordinance that protected Cincinnatians from discrimination in employment, housing, or credit on "the basis of age, dependency obligations, gender, handicap, marital status, national origin, neighborhood, personal appearance, personal sexuality, political affiliation, pregnancy, prior arrest or conviction, race or religious affiliation" got bogged down in city council committee hearings. It would take another fourteen years before city council would pass a human rights ordinance.

- The commission was publicly embarrassed after its investigation justifying the firing of an employee in the city's planning department was determined to be a clear case of discrimination by the Equal Employment Opportunity Commission, the Ohio Civil Rights Commission, and the federal Department of Housing and Urban Development.

- Councilman Thomas Brush called for a complete overhaul of the commission because of "a general dissatisfaction with the assistance CHRC was giving council." He added, "I felt they lacked a sense of direction." In subsequent changes led by Brush, the commission's budget became subject to council approval of individual program elements instead of a flat allowance from the city.

- After the deciding vote was cast by Helen Hinckley, a new appointee to the CHRC board, that opposed home rule over the city's civil service system, Mayor Gerald Springer revoked her appointment to the commission.

- Chief Myron Leistler publicly criticized the commission's handling of citizen complaints against the police. Noting some complaints were misplaced by the CHRC for months, Leistler said, "The CHRC seems to have no rationale on how to handle these complaints. What they do is pass them on to us and pass the results we get on to the complaining people as if they had obtained them."

- The commission's effectiveness in dealing with police-community relations was also criticized by Chief Leistler and some council members. The CHRC's board chair, Donald Mooney, responded:

> The city council and the administration have put us in the rather difficult position of, on the one hand, accepting and processing and investigating the complaints of citizens (against the police division), and on the other, of trying to improve relations between citizens and the police [division]. Often, when we are processing a complaint against a police officer the [division] thinks we're anti-police. Then, when we go to them with positive ways we think we can improve police-community relations, they're suspect [*sic*] of our motives.

One suggestion to resolve this conflict was to contract with Legal Aid to take over the CHRC's complaint investigation duties. After the killing of three Cincinnati police officers in nine months between the summer of 1978 and the spring of 1979, a panel led by Lawrence Hawkins was appointed to make recommendations on how to improve police-community relations. All the recommendations of the Hawkins Commission were accepted except the one suggesting a community oversight board to monitor police activities. Instead, a professionally staffed Office of Municipal Investigations was established to "resolve complaints against police officers and other city personnel for abuse of authority and unnecessary use of force." Thus the CHRC was relieved of its dilemma of both investigating the police and promoting good police-community relations, but lost another of its core functions.

Adding to the general dissension was the appointment of white attorney Donald Mooney as the CHRC board chair at the recommendation of the previous chair, Bernard Rosenberg. Some board members led by Ernie Waits favored the appointment of black attorney Dwight Tillery. Waits accused Mayor Springer of having a "plantation mentality" and suspected there was "a Watergate conspiracy" underlying the appointment. Tillery, who claimed not to want the position, nonetheless noted that "there was talk of a conspiracy, a 'Watergate' mentality, on the main issue—which was the clandestine way the chair appointment was made." Mooney would serve as the 1979–80 board chair, but the turmoil within the CHRC board did not abate, and city council remained displeased with the agency. In the final year of the decade the commission's budget allocation from the city was reduced by 27 percent.

Despite this political and administrative turmoil, the CHRC staff continued to carry out the core functions of the agency. A survey of annual reports issued in the latter half of the 1970s shows the CHRC training municipal employees in the city's affirmative action program, providing training to police recruit classes, participating in activities of the Open Housing Coalition, working with public schools to handle grievances, and assisting with community organization in Appalachian neighborhoods. "Field Activities" staffers worked with community councils, providing liaison with city hall for eight predominantly black neighborhoods. In addition to the ongoing urban Appalachian initiative, the CHRC began reaching out to "women, the handicapped, and the aging." Moreover, the Cincinnati police division revised its firearms policy "in several critical areas" with advice from the CHRC and the Ministerial Alliance. This occurred in part because Chief Leistler agreed with the CHRC that the 1978 shooting of seventeen-year-old Herman Beasley in Winton Terrace was a violation of police procedure. By 1979 the commission had worked with the police division to recruit minority candidates and to reestablish the division's police-community relations section. Fortunately, the turmoil within the CHRC and the political climate in Cincinnati that made it so difficult for the agency during the decade was not reflective of the national situation.

5

Dealing with Instability

The 1980s

In many ways the 1980s were promising years for race relations in the United States. The decade saw the popularization of the terms African American and black rather than Negro or colored as ethnic references. In October 1980, President Jimmy Carter signed legislation establishing the Boston African American National Historic Site, which included the oldest black church in America. In the same year Congress passed legislation extending the Voting Rights Act for twenty-five years. Two years later Rev. Jesse Jackson waged the first major campaign by an African American seeking the Democratic Party nomination for president. In 1984, Vanessa Williams was selected as the first African American Miss America, astronaut Guion "Guy" S. Bluford Jr. became the first African American in space, and the National Rainbow Coalition was established by Rev. Jesse Jackson. In January 1986, Martin Luther King Day was officially observed as a federal holiday. Congress passed the Civil Rights Restoration Act in 1988, which expanded nondiscrimination laws to private industry, and in 1989 Colin Powell became the first African American to be appointed chairman of the Joint Chiefs of Staff.

The only major civil disturbance during the decade were the 1980 Miami riots. Sometimes referred to as the McDuffie riots, they began following the acquittal of four white Miami-Dade police officers charged with the death of thirty-three-year-old Arthur McDuffie, an African American. Following the trial, a crowd estimated at over 5,000 people gathered for a peaceful protest that soon turned violent. Ultimately 3,500 Florida National Guard troops were called in to quell the disturbance; the final outcome was 18 people killed, 350 injured, 600 arrested, and property damage of more than $100 million.

A 1974 suit brought against the Cincinnati Public Schools by the NAACP was finally settled in 1985 by providing alternative, or "magnet," schools open to all students as a means to achieve integration. A fourteen-member task force was established to monitor the progress of the plan under a judge's supervision.

I n Cincinnati, civil rights progress was made in the hiring of police officers. In 1980 the Department of Justice commenced an action against the city, alleging that the Cincinnati Police Division and the U.S. Civil Service Commission "engaged in hiring and promoting practices that discriminated against blacks and women in violation of Title VII." Following more than a year of negotiations, a consent decree was adopted establishing "a long term goal of hiring and promoting blacks and women in approximate proportion of qualified blacks and women in Cincinnati's work force."

Coming out of a decade of city hall sniping and criticism of its activities and leadership, the CHRC faced a period of turnover sandwiched between two periods of stability. The end of the 1970s saw calls for restructuring the CHRC board by members of city council, newspaper editorials calling for the CHRC's board and staff to resume working in the background and discontinue making themselves the center of attention, and a highly critical confidential letter from city manager William Donaldson to council members claiming the agency had harmed rather than improved community and police relations.

Late in 1982, Thomas Garner resigned after serving eight years as executive director, citing differences with commission chair Rev. James Milton. Marcia Hall-Craig, followed by George Penn, would fill the role of executive director during a three-year period until Dr. W. Monty Whitney was appointed to that post in early 1986. Throughout the

1980s the CHRC continued to be the target of city council members, administrators in city hall, and individuals across Cincinnati, leading to a loss of standing within city hall and the larger community. In a 1986 *Cincinnati Enquirer* article, reporter Allen Howard described the agency's diminishment, noting it "has had a rugged and controversial existence. It seems that every time a politician needed a scapegoat, CHRC has been the target." Howard reported that the CHRC continued to lose its authority over program areas. "First its housing contract was taken over by Housing Opportunity Made Equal." Next, "the CHRC's investigative powers of city agencies and employees were taken over by the Office of Municipal Investigations."

At the time of his resignation Thomas Garner had served fourteen years on the CHRC staff, the final eight as executive director. Before leaving, Garner and some of his staff, including Arzell Nelson, began working with members of the gay and lesbian community to address complaints of gay bashing and police intolerance. Although focused on race relations, the CHRC held a "vision to be an umbrella for all marginalized groups" according to Tedd Good, a gay activist during the 1980s. The CHRC staff advised gay leaders on how to form a cohesive activist movement and acted as a go-between with city council and police leadership. Eventually the work and support of the CHRC during the 1980s would lead to city council adopting a human rights ordinance in 1992 providing protections for all Cincinnati's marginal-group citizens, including urban Appalachians, gays, and lesbians.

In the last year of Garner's tenure, in addition to its usual activities of sponsoring workshops and seminars and handling citizen complaints, the CHRC staff designed and implemented a successful Advanced Control Techniques training program for police officers. The CHRC also convened a police-community relations advisory panel. Although the establishment of the panel created some heated political infighting, it eventually became a successful program and served as a forerunner for the appointment of a full-time police-community relations staff member in 1988.

There were few notable accomplishments beyond the usual activities during the three years Marcia Hall-Craig and George Penn served as executive directors, due in part to the short period each was in office. Hall-Craig, a doctoral student at the University of Cincinnati, was appointed in January 1983 but left the position after a year to take a similar job in Fort Worth, Texas. George Penn, who had been deputy director of the Citizens Committee on Youth for the previous six years, stepped in as the CHRC's director from 1984 to 1985.

Dr. W. Monty Whitney, the first psychologist to hold the position, was appointed executive director in March 1986 and would serve until 1991. Allen Howard reported in the *Cincinnati Enquirer* that Whitney "may be taking over a mere skeleton of the original CHRC . . . but the primary needs are still there, including the need to help fortify the harmony that was threatened 43 years ago." Whitney was associate director of Seven Hills Neighborhood Houses and had served on the faculties of the University of Cincinnati and Southern University, a historically black institution in Baton Rouge, Louisiana. In Howard's article Whitney expressed confidence that he, his staff and CHRC board members could "direct the organization toward achieving the goals for which it was created." Whitney went on to note,

> Sure, CHRC has been the brunt of criticism, the scapegoat, and even now because it is not a revenue producing agency, its functions are always circumspect. The important thing about CHRC is that it is a mediator, the communicator between agencies of the city and also the various entities of the community. Quietly, it has always functioned that way. The agency has not received notoriety because its job was to prevent a crisis before it started.

Although Whitney was candid in his evaluation of the CHRC's status, the agency continued to pursue its mission in spite of the pressures it faced. Soon after Whitney's appointment, the CHRC published the second *Social Areas of Cincinnati* report by Michael Maloney. Based on the 1980 census, the report had become an essential tool used by Cincinnati area social agencies in program planning and service delivery to the city's residents. The CHRC also initiated the Youth Crime Intervention Project in collaboration with the University of Cincinnati Alcoholism Clinic and the Cincinnati Youth Collaborative.

Throughout the decade the CHRC continued its program and training activities with the Cincinnati Public Schools, the city's police division, fire division, as well as several city departments such as Public Works and the Health Department. Program activities also were extended beyond the city limits to meet the needs of organizations such as the Great Rivers Girl Scout Council, the Black-Jewish Coalition, and People Working Cooperatively (an agency founded by former CHRC staffer Charles "Chuck" Hirt). Other public organizations outside the city—such as the Norwood Police Department, North College Hill School District, and Xavier University Safety Department—were provided with CHRC services. The process of creating the new Winton Hills School District through the merger of the Greenhills and Forest Park School Districts also benefited from the services of the CHRC staff.

Under Whitney's leadership the CHRC worked to address youth and crime issues in the city. In 1987 it initiated the Youth Crime Prevention Project and the following year established the West End Community Adolescent Priorities Project, modeled after the YCPP. Despite these initiatives, concern about youth crime problems throughout the city remained. The agency also tried to calm the waters when neo-Nazis and the White American Skinheads demonstrated on Fountain Square and elsewhere in the city.

Susan Noonan was hired by Whitney in 1988 as the first police-community relations staff member. Noonan, who held a graduate degree from the University of Cincinnati's School of Criminal Justice, would work for the CHRC for the next twelve years, including her role as acting director from 1998 to 2000. After Noonan was hired she quickly found the city hall political scene surprisingly difficult: "We sort of existed with city council. CHRC was always looked upon as the stepchild and funding was hard to get."

1. *Left to right:* Robert Stargel, Marshall Bragdon, Eugene Sparrow, S. Arthur Spiegel. (Courtesy of Archives and Rare Books, University of Cincinnati)

2. Danny Litwhiler and Jackie Robinson at a 1948 MFRC promotional event. (Courtesy of Cincinnati Museum Center—Cincinnati History Library and Archives)

3. David McPheeters, assistant director, executive director of the Cincinnati Human Relations Commission. (Courtesy of Michael E. Maloney)

4. Virginia Coffey, assistant director, executive director of the CHRC. (Courtesy of Cincinnati Museum Center— Cincinnati History Library and Archives)

5. Virginia Coffey speaking to the 1968 Cincinnati Police Division recruit class. (Courtesy of Archives and Rare Books, University of Cincinnati)

6. *Left to right:* Thomas Garner, Judge S. Arthur Spiegel, Virginia Coffey, and Judge Robert Black at the 1972 CHRC annual meeting. (Courtesy of Archives and Rare Books, University of Cincinnati)

7. Thomas Garner with Virginia Coffey at the 1973 CHRC annual meeting. (Courtesy of Archives and Rare Books, University of Cincinnati)

8. Stevie Wonder at a 1986 CHRC Get Out the Vote event. (Courtesy of Cincinnati Museum Center—Cincinnati History Library and Archives)

9. Dr. W. Monty Whitney, executive director of the CHRC. (Courtesy of Archives and Rare Books, University of Cincinnati)

10. CHRC executive director Arzell Nelson. (Courtesy of Michael E. Maloney)

11. Susan Noonan, CHRC staff member and acting executive director. (Courtesy of Archives and Rare Books, University of Cincinnati)

12. CHRC executive director Dr. W. Monty Whitney, Cincinnati mayor Charlie Luken, CHRC board chair Mark A. Vander Laan. (Courtesy of Archives and Rare Books, University of Cincinnati)

13. One of the CHRC Study Circles organized after the 2001 riots. (Courtesy of Archives and Rare Books, University of Cincinnati)

14. Judge S. Arthur Spiegel (*center, back to camera*) swears in the 2003 CHRC board. (Courtesy of Archives and Rare Books, University of Cincinnati)

15. Michael Maloney, Virginia Coffey, Stuart Faber, and Louise Spiegel at an Urban Appalachian Council recognition event. (Courtesy of Thomas E. Wagner)

16. CHRC executive director Cecil Thomas. (Courtesy of Archives and Rare Books, University of Cincinnati)

17. *Left to right:* CHRC board chair Arthur Schriberg, Cincinnati mayor Charlie Luken, and CHRC executive director Cecil Thomas. (Courtesy of Archives and Rare Books, University of Cincinnati)

18. *Left to right:* Judge S. Arthur Spiegel, Sister Jean Patrice Harrington, and John Pepper. (Courtesy of Archives and Rare Books, University of Cincinnati)

19. Cincinnati council member Paul Booth with the 2002 Elthelrie Harper Award winner, Sgt. Sylvia Ranaghan. (Courtesy of Archives and Rare Books, University of Cincinnati)

20. CHRC executive director Ericka King-Betts. (Courtesy of Dr. Ericka King-Betts)

6

Starting the Decade Well,

Ending with Difficulty

The 1990s

In 1990, President George H. W. Bush signed into law the Americans with Disabilities Act, providing comprehensive civil rights protection for people with disabilities. The following year, the Civil Rights Act of 1991 was passed by Congress and signed by President Bush. Thurgood Marshall, the first African American to serve on the Supreme Court, resigned and Clarence Thomas was sworn in as an associate justice.

There were few civil disturbances until the beating of African American Rodney King in Los Angeles. Videos of the arrest and beating of King were shown repeatedly on television news shows. In April 1992 the four LAPD officers tried for the beating were acquitted, sparking riots in which fifty-two people were killed and several thousand were injured. They were the largest riots in the United States since the 1967 Detroit riot and the largest in California since the 1965 Watts riots. One incident during the LA riots was the attack by at least six African Americans on Reginald

Denny, a white truck driver. Filmed by a helicopter television crew, the beating of Denny further inflamed racial tensions.

Soon after being sworn into office in 1993, President Bill Clinton signed an executive order that became known as the "don't ask, don't tell, don't pursue" policy eliminating the ban on gays and lesbians from serving in the military.

In 1995 the Supreme Court ruled on two cases that limited the use of race in government decisions, especially in creating congressional districts that favor minorities. The primary civil rights actions during the latter half of the decade occurred in courtrooms where several cases regarding the use of racial data in setting congressional districts, applications of the Americans with Disabilities Act, and gender issues were adjudicated. In October 1996, African Americans gathered in Washington, DC, for the Million Man March. Locally, the Cincinnati Enquirer *published a six-part series based on over 350 interviews with black and white residents titled "A Polite Silence: Race Relations in Cincinnati."*

A s the decade opened, the CHRC had much-needed leadership continuity in Dr. Monty Whitney and a strong team in staff members Arzell Nelson and Susan Noonan. The agency's Back on the Block youth summer jobs program and its expanded Community Relations Monitors project would see success over the next several years.

Back on the Block, established in collaboration with the Citizens Committee on Youth and the Cincinnati Recreation Commission, would eventually become a full program under the CHRC. The program focused on key neighborhoods and provided job opportunities and recreation activities for youth. A 1997 review of Back on the Block described it as an effort by the agencies to develop a "coordinated system of services." A Youth Steering Committee was appointed after a study found that the "root causes of the detrimental behavior of youth between the ages of 13–21 [are] historical disenfranchisement, poverty, discrimination, inadequate education and skill levels, damaged self-esteem and thwarted aspirations." Summer youth workers under the supervision of the CHRC staff organized recreation activities in collaboration with the Recreation Commission, including a very popular talent festival at the Sawyer Point pavilion. One special feature in 1997 was a scuba diving and snorkeling program at several neighborhood swimming pools.

The Community Relations Monitors program hired off-duty Recreation Commission staff to be available during events where large numbers of youth were likely to be present. Working under the direction of the city's safety director and the police division, the monitors were there to help defuse disturbances and problem situations. "The police were really happy to have us there because we were the buffer between them getting into altercations with a lot of the youth," said Noonan. Although constantly under pressure from officials at city hall and limited in budget, the CHRC was not facing any major political efforts to close or reorganize it during this time. Unfortunately, it would be a different story by the end of the decade.

The CHRC's efforts to fulfill its mission experienced a minor setback in 1992 when Dr. Whitney resigned as executive director to take a position at Morehouse College, in Atlanta. A *Cincinnati Enquirer* article about his departure commented: "In recent months—particularly after the Los Angeles riots—[the CHRC] has been in the spotlight as the citywide agency charged with diffusing tension between the races. Meanwhile Whitney has been critical of the lack of resources to do the job. 'Human relations covers a wide gamut of areas,' he said." Whitney further stated that the pressure on the agency was not the reason he was leaving, rather that his new position was a highly desired job. Arzell Nelson, a twenty-year staff member, was appointed interim head of the agency and soon after became executive director.

A Cincinnati native with experience in human relations work, Nelson assumed the leadership of the CHRC at one of the calmer periods in its controversial existence. When asked about the CHRC's mission, Nelson replied, "You have to constantly deal with the institutional issue. But at the same time, we've got to create a spirit in our community that [makes] people want to come together. We have to build bridges on all levels in Cincinnati, and we have to call the leadership to task to be more assertive on these issues. . . . And it's going to take resources to do that."

Susan Noonan reflected on Nelson's years as director: "Arzell and I worked unbelievably well together. He taught me so much because he had grown up in Cincinnati. He had experienced discrimination himself even within his own family. . . . Arzell taught me how better to deal with people when there was conflict. He was just so laid back. He allowed his staff to do whatever they were able—they had open access.

He was a great director." Two well-established programs continued to be effective under Nelson's leadership—upon his retirement from the CHRC in 1998, Nelson stated that during his time with the agency he was proudest of the Back on the Block and Community Relations Monitors programs.

The Community Relations Monitors (CRM) program was successful in reducing tensions between police and community residents, especially in volatile situations where youth were likely to congregate. Susan Noonan, who directed the program, described working at one of the Jazz Festival weekends. "We worked the whole weekend because there were many African American teens downtown. . . . We were able to be a buffer between the police and the kids." Noonan also described how the CRM program extended into other areas where rising racial tensions could create conflicts. "[We started] going into neighborhoods where there was a problem, whether it was a racial problem or an ethnic problem. We went to Roselawn when the Orthodox Jews were being stoned—rocks thrown at them by some of the new African American teens who had moved in. We did a lot of mediation in neighborhoods that way."

The *Cincinnati Post* reported in 1993 on a CRM neighborhood intervention in Lower Price Hill in response to a Christmas night fight between black and white residents. The incident started when a group of people began throwing snowballs and then bricks at an apartment rented by a black family. "We're getting together to see what really happened and see who the instigators are," Susan Noonan told a reporter on the scene. "Without a doubt this is a racial incident. Tomorrow is the beginning of what we hope is some communication."

Community Relations Monitors also worked when the Ku Klux Klan and other white supremacy groups rallied on Cincinnati's Fountain Square. In one incident, Noonan found herself between police on horseback and a falling KKK cross. "Fear is usually something we don't think about until the next day," she told a *Cincinnati Enquirer* reporter. After Noonan left the CHRC, the Community Relations Monitors program experienced a decline, she said, because "the Safety Director did not trust someone else to run it."

Noonan described the Back on the Block program as "one of the highlights of the period when I was there." The CHRC hired college students for summer work in neighborhoods, usually where there was also a community recreation center or playground. "They would just start talking to neighborhood kids. They would get them to come into the rec centers. We planned talent contests, we planned basketball contests, and we did field trips. What they were doing was developing relationships. They just got out there and talked in the neighborhoods. . . . It was a wonderful program." The program continued for about six years but lack of resources put a drain on staff and other programs. "It just ended," said Noonan, "it took so much time and effort."

Despite opposition from some citizens, the CHRC intensified its efforts to support gay rights. The agency sponsored a series of panel discussions and other activities to promote inclusion of sexual orientation and people with disabilities in the city's antidiscrimination and human rights law. A proposal to amend the law to extend protection to age, gender, disability, and sexual orientation was being debated by city council. The CHRC successfully provided a channel for proponents of the amendment to be heard, and the amendment was adopted by city council.

The CHRC also organized the Inter-Ethnic Council of Greater Cincinnati, a group of twenty-eight different ethnic groups. Susan Noonan described the organization as having

> Asians, Hispanics, Indians, English, Scottish—we had every group you can imagine. We brought everyone together. We had informational programs. It became sort of the umbrella group when there was any kind of ethnic problem in any neighborhood. . . . We worked with every group you can imagine including the gay/lesbian population. We became really active when the hate crime legislation first went through.

Unfortunately, after Nelson and then Noonan left the CHRC, the Inter-Ethnic Council "just sort of dissolved."

In 1997 the CHRC collaborated with several other organizations, local corporations, and the Cincinnati Reds to sponsor Jackie Robinson Day to recognize the famous Brooklyn Dodger player who broke the color line in professional baseball. The celebration commemorated the fiftieth anniversary of Robinson's first appearance in Cincinnati, often considered a turning point in his acceptance by major-league players and fans. The CHRC was also instrumental in establishing the Chuck Harmon Youth Baseball Fund in collaboration with the Greater

Cincinnati Chamber of Commerce and the Cincinnati Reds. Harmon was the first African American to play for the Reds; the fund was created to recognize his contributions to the Reds and to major league baseball by raising funds to support youth baseball teams in inner-city neighborhoods.

After nearly ten years of stable leadership by Monty Whitney and Arzell Nelson, the CHRC was once again confronted with a serious challenge to its existence. The first evidence of the coming turmoil was a statement by Michael W. Hawkins, chair of the CHRC's board, in an article about Arzell Nelson's retirement: "Anytime you have change it always gives you the opportunity to think more out of the box and look for new opportunities—is there a better way to do it?"

The threat to the agency came from an old nemesis, city council, and was similar to several previous ones. Over its history, the city administration, council members, and individual citizens frequently questioned the CHRC's structure, usefulness, and purpose. David McPheeters was suspended and then fired when he was not in the city during the 1967 riot. In 1968 there were open discussions about bringing the agency closer to the mayor and city council. In 1978 it was recommended that the CHRC be restructured and be given subpoena powers to investigate human relations complaints against city departments. The CHRC was indeed restructured but its duty to review contracts to ensure compliance with the city's minority goals was moved elsewhere. In the 1980s the agency's responsibility for investigating housing complaints and complaints against city employees was transferred to other agencies. With a history of constant attacks, the newest challenge to its existence should not have been unexpected.

Commissioners also began open discussions about ways to reorganize the agency to better focus its activities. "I think there has been a feeling for some time that we have not had a good sense of what we are trying to accomplish," said commission member Susan Livensparger. "Our effort wasn't any elaborate plan to restructure. It really was to get the agency more focused to do a reasonable number of things so that it can be effective." Council member Charlie Winburn, a longtime critic of the CHRC, noted, "I can't measure their performance. We need to either give it a focus or eliminate it." Susan Noonan, serving as the acting director, defended the agency: "I think we serve a purpose that no other agency or department serves. We are that last resort for many people—not that we can handle every complaint that comes in here."

The challenge to the CHRC came from three council members—Minette Cooper, Dwight Tillery, and Charlie Winburn—who introduced a motion to revamp the agency. According to a *Cincinnati Post* article, the CHRC would become responsible (1) for enforcing the city's minority and female-business set aside programs, (2) investigating complaints of discrimination, (3) monitoring the city's hiring, testing, and promotion system, and (4) police-community relations. The reorganization would also move the Office of Contract Compliance and Office of Municipal Investigations to the CHRC.

This unsolicited proposal provoked all fifteen members of the CHRC board to resign. In a letter to Mayor Roxanne Qualls, CHRC board chair, Gwen Robinson, stated, "We have yet to receive a copy of the proposal nor were we asked for input or suggestions. . . . For some reason, which we believe to be political and self-motivated, we were left out of the process. We felt we have been ignored as board members and insulted as volunteers for the city." In a separate letter to council members, Hawkins, then the board's vice chair, wrote that he could "no longer in good faith serve on an agency which is so adversely impacted by politicians who have not been able to develop a meaningful and consistent approach to human relations. They have their own agenda and I choose not to be a part of it and their games."

Tillery claimed he was "baffled by the resignations," and Winburn stated that the resignations were "a great opportunity for City council to reinvent or re-engineer this entire agency." About a week after the en masse resignations, several CHRC board members notified council that they wished to continue as members of the commission. The remaining board members elected Ernest J. Waits Jr. as chair and confirmed Susan Noonan's appointment as acting executive director.

The Cooper, Tillery, and Winburn challenge to the CHRC came to an abrupt end in August 1998, when city attorney Fay Dupuis wrote a report to city council indicating the duties it was planning to transfer to the CHRC could not be delegated because the private agency was not "an arm of city government." Additionally, the council had no authority to change the number and appointment process of the CHRC board. The resolution by the three council members was also questioned by several civic leaders, including Dr. Milton Hinton, president of the Cincinnati chapter of the NAACP. Hinton's letter to city council, as reported in a *Cincinnati Post* article, called the plan "ambitious" but said that "the goal of the proposal was unclear." Therefore the NAACP, Hinton stated, was not in a position to support the proposal.

The last two years of the decade were by comparison uneventful. Under Noonan's temporary leadership the agency continued to provide several programs to enhance human relations in Cincinnati. It received belated praise for its efforts to address the violence that accompanied the 1997 Coors Lite Riverfront Stadium Festival. The Back on the Block and Community Relations Monitors programs were still active, and efforts to strengthen police-community relations were ongoing. The agency also continued to provide training programs for police, school teachers, and other human service professionals and to support diverse community groups. Susan Noonan served until early 2000, when Cecil Thomas was appointed executive director.

7

Containing the Turmoil

The 2000s

At the national level, a Supreme Court decision in 2003 confirmed the right of higher-education institutions to use race as a factor in decisions about admissions. In 2005, twenty-one years after three civil rights workers were killed in Mississippi, the leader of the group responsible was convicted for the murders. Senator Edward Kennedy proposed the Civil Rights Act of 2008, which included provisions to ensure that federal funds were not used to subsidize discrimination, introduced new regulations governing age discrimination, and instituted accountability for other violations of civil rights. Barack Obama's election as president in 2008 promised to usher in a new era in minority and majority group relations.

The largest civil disturbance in the United States since the 1992 Los Angeles riots occurred in Cincinnati in 2001. A number of injuries were reported but there were no deaths attributed to the disturbance; nine hundred people were arrested for vandalism and breaking the curfew during four nights of unrest. Damage to private property was estimated at more than $3 million and direct costs to the city at nearly

$2 million. A subsequent boycott of the city resulted in an estimated $10 million loss for the region's entertainment and convention businesses.

The riots were triggered by the police shooting of Timothy Thomas, an unarmed black man, on April 7, 2001. The deaths of two black men at the hands of the police in the months before the shooting of Thomas had already raised tensions between the black community and the Cincinnati Police Division (CPD). In the six years before Thomas's death, moreover, fifteen black men had been killed in encounters with the CPD. An analysis of the causes of the Cincinnati riots found that only three of the deaths, including Thomas's, were strictly due to police action. Even so, racial tension nationally and in Cincinnati inflamed large numbers of people.

The 2001 riots were centered in Over-the-Rhine, a predominantly black and formerly urban Appalachian neighborhood just north of the city's business district. Two days after Thomas's death a large crowd gathered outside city hall to protest his and the deaths of the other black men at the hands of CPD officers. Thomas's mother and several black community leaders demanded that city council release the CPD's report on the shooting, but the police chief refused to do so until the investigation was completed. A crowd prevented council members from leaving city hall for over three hours. The crowd, growing by the hour, then moved a few blocks north, to CPD headquarters in Over-the-Rhine, where the protesters, confronted by police officers in riot gear, began throwing stones at the officers and the building. Eventually, the rioters were dispersed and a night of relative quiet ensued.

The following day a peaceful crowd in Over-the-Rhine began walking to the central business district. Once downtown, the marchers became unruly and began throwing rocks and bricks, overturning vendor carts, and looting stores. It was reported that some whites were attacked by young black men. Hamilton County Sheriff's Office deputies were called in for assistance when the disturbance spread to Avondale and Walnut Hills, two other predominantly African American communities. On the evening of April 11 rioting again broke out in the downtown business district, with extensive vandalism and looting. The next day Mayor Charlie Luken declared an emergency, established a curfew, and called in 125 Ohio State Highway Patrol officers to assist the CPD and sheriff's deputies in maintaining order. On the day of Timothy Thomas's funeral, a large group marched peacefully in his memory, although a smaller group broke away and confronted police at a downtown intersection. This minor disturbance signaled an end to the riots.

The city was soon boycotted by several groups who canceled scheduled conventions, and some businesses closed because of damage. The officer who killed Thomas was tried and acquitted of negligent homicide but resigned from the CPD. The city signed a court-supervised collaborative agreement in 2002 to improve police relations with minority communities, review and revise use-of-force protocols, and study community policing procedures. Gentrification of Over-the-Rhine seemed to accelerate after the disturbances in the neighborhood as property prices dropped dramatically and speculators began moving in to develop upscale housing and restaurants.

The CHRC entered the decade still under threat of dissolution from several sources. A city council–commissioned study of the CHRC initiated in 1999 and released in January 2000 brought out both critics and supporters of the organization. The authors of the report, according to the *Cincinnati Enquirer,* criticized the agency for being "virtually unknown and unseen" within the city. Supporters of the commission argued that "it has become victimized by political whims and stripped of its funding by city council." Former executive director Thomas Garner told city council members during a hearing that in times of civil unrest "there is no question of our effectiveness." He further noted that when there is no strife, the CHRC is usually targeted for budget cuts. Commission chair Ernest Waits Jr. wrote a letter to council members stating,

> It is my honest and sincere opinion that the [CHRC] has been the object of politically engineered manipulation. . . . It is hard to visualize any possible constructive purpose to be served by beheading the staff of the commission, not allowing the replacement of the director and freezing the appointment of additional board members and then order a study of the effectiveness of the now crippled agency.

The 2000 report did not recommend dissolving the CHRC but pointed out that it should be restructured to change the way it provided "human relations services." The authors proposed a "bold disconnect" from city hall and that it be established as an independent agency with its own budget, staff, and facilities to create a presence in all the city's neighborhoods. Discussion about the CHRC's future role and mission continued well into the early months of 2000, with some critics on city council wanting to end all of its funding while others sought to change its mission. In December of that year city council voted to accept several recommendations to reorganize the agency. One recommendation was to have the commission report directly to the mayor, who would appoint board members and submit a budget to city council. Another recommendation called for narrowing the mission to strictly improving human relations and forgoing all other duties.

Early in 2000 board chair Waits called Cecil Thomas, a twenty-five-year veteran of the Cincinnati Police Division, and asked if he would consider applying for the vacant executive director position. After graduating from Withrow High School, Thomas had joined the police cadet program at the University of Cincinnati. The cooperative education program there allowed students to earn an associate degree in police technology while serving during alternate terms as a police cadet. At the time Thomas was sworn in there were 48 African Americans among the city's 958 police officers.

Thomas had been an activist during his years on the police force, pushing for less discrimination toward blacks and women in the promotion process and assignment of duties. The efforts of Thomas and others had led to a consent decree in 1980 to increase the number of women and blacks on the force, open special assignments (e.g., undercover), and improve opportunities for promotions. In 1997, Thomas became president of the Sentinel Police Association, an organization of the black police officers in the CPD, a role that made him much more visible in the community. He recalled in an interview, "I started to see a number of incidents. Even before 1997 there were a lot of incidents involving police-citizen contacts. . . . One of the complaints being levied against the police was the indiscriminate stopping of African Americans for no real reason whatsoever, other than to use the stop as a pretext for further investigations." In 1999, Thomas compiled a study of complaints filed with the Citizens Review Board and submitted it to the U.S. Justice Department, urging it to intervene in Cincinnati because, he said, "we're on the verge of some form of civil unrest." The riots of 2001 proved that Thomas was keenly aware of minority concerns in Cincinnati.

When Waits asked Thomas to become the CHRC's executive director, his first response was, "Wait a minute, you want me to leave my job and become director of the Human Relations Commission?" "Just think about it," was Waits's reply. Thomas agreed to think about it but soon learned that the city was seriously thinking about closing the agency. "Why would I leave my job and go to a sinking ship?" Thomas asked. Waits replied, "We believe that you have the strength to bring it back to life based on the work you are doing." After some consideration, Thomas agreed to accept the position and in April 2000 was appointed acting executive director.

Cecil Thomas's appointment by the CHRC board was not well received by some city council members. Within hours of the announcement the council voted not to give the CHRC any additional money and strongly questioned its role in and benefit to the city. "All I heard from them is that they want a clear direction. That gives me and the board something to work on, to give them that direction. I assure you the Human Relations Commission is just as valuable today as it was yesterday, and as it will most certainly be tomorrow," Thomas announced. He promised to focus on the agency's internal organization and to build better relationships with city council and the Cincinnati Police Division. Mayor Charlie Luken objected to the interim appointment while the agency was under review, and council members Phil Heimlich and Charlie Winburn spoke in favor of defunding the commission. Other council members favored keeping the agency and requested that the commissioners and executive director present the council with a list of goals. The president of the police union criticized the appointment, saying Thomas had "a very polarizing personality." Thomas responded by saying that he was committed to improving human relations in the city.

The CHRC was not only vulnerable to actions by city council but also to threats to its existence from other directions. Thomas remembered that he had been in office less than a month or two when he was told that a prominent citizen and lobbyist wanted to meet him. At a luncheon meeting the individual told Thomas, "I want your Community Relations Monitors program." The program that had operated so successfully under Susan Noonan had been revitalized by Thomas as one of his first actions as acting director. Thomas replied, "I am not going to give that up." The lobbyist's response was, "The CHRC's going to be gone and you may as well give it up. I've got the votes [in city council] to get it if you don't voluntarily give it up." Thomas later learned that internal CHRC politics was at play here; with the agency at risk of being closed, a former staff member was trying to establish a new agency using the Community Relations Monitors program as its basis. This new organization was intended to operate under the auspices of a youth services agency.

Thomas made the politically astute move of showing up at the next city council meeting and requesting to speak during the open session for public comments. He told council members that the CHRC had a successful Community Relations Monitors program and an individual had stated that he "has the votes to get my program. . . . I just want you to know that I will be fighting that very strongly. CHRC needs that program because it's in the community." Mayor Charlie Luken assured Thomas that no one had approached his office with such a proposal. Although several council members looked very uncomfortable, according to Thomas, "nobody would dare touch it." Several months later the lobbyist told Thomas, "you're the first one who's ever done that to me. I really respect you." The activist demonstrated his respect by supporting Thomas in his subsequent political campaigns.

With the threat of closing the CHRC disarmed, Thomas focused on improving the agency:

> Then I began my work to really begin to rebuild the structure and I needed to, at the time, fashion it around police-community relations, youth and things that were going on with them. . . . We were having problems with, what you see today, youth beating up people. Youth going to events . . . and raging through, hitting people, acting all crazy.

Thomas's year-long efforts to rebuild the CHRC seemed to be working when the riots in April 2001 brought racial chaos to the city. Thomas recalled:

> The tensions were high between citizens and police. My role as head of the commission was to find ways to reduce that tension. I kept going to city council, saying to them, you've got to give me more resources to get people into the community to let people vent their frustrations. . . . I had my monitors in the Over-the-Rhine area and they said it's getting really hot down there.

In Thomas's view the best means to reduce tensions in the neighborhoods was through the Community Relations Monitors program.

> The CRMs were former employees of recreation centers or current recreation center employees. They were also baseball coaches, basketball coaches, football coaches who interacted with these kids on a daily basis in the neighborhoods . . . they have a personal relationship. If you are going to solve the problem, you're going to have to use the method by which you established personal relationships.

Protest over the shooting of Timothy Thomas brought Cecil Thomas and his staff onto the streets to try to calm the situation. Their efforts did not go unnoticed by city hall. In his January 2002 State of the City address, as reported in the *Cincinnati Enquirer,* Mayor Charlie Luken credited the CHRC as one of the organizations "helping to improve race relations in Cincinnati." A month after the riots, councilmember Phil Heimlich still questioned the CHRC's $460,000 budget request but commended Thomas's outreach activities.

Interestingly, neither Cecil Thomas nor anyone else associated with the CHRC was chosen to serve on the privately funded task force appointed by Mayor Luken in June 2001 to "identify and implement policies and programs to eliminate disparities in the justice system and create a more positive relationship between police officers and the people they serve." The task force, named Cincinnati Community Action Now, or Cincinnati CAN, included citizens from a variety of backgrounds. With Ross Love, Thomas Cody, and Rev. Damon Lynch III serving as cochairs of the group, the task force organized itself into six teams to address specific areas of concern. Cincinnati CAN soon fell into the typical political maneuvering within city hall. For instance, Mayor Luken later removed Reverend Lynch, citing a conflict of interest between Lynch's community activities and the work of the task force. Eventually, Cincinnati CAN issued a report with several recommendations for programs to improve race relations in the city.

Thomas and the CHRC staff did not wait for a committee to study the issues. Within a month of the riots, Thomas was walking the streets of Over-the-Rhine "trying to gauge the temperature of residents who live in Cincinnati's most impoverished inner-city neighborhood," he said in a *Cincinnati Enquirer* article. "The temperature is very unstable. There's no one that's really come in and committed to an effort that's going to effect change." The CHRC staff quickly reached out with community programs. A Day in the Park, cosponsored by the CHRC and the Cincinnati Police Division, hosted over two thousand youth in a six-hour program in several Cincinnati parks. "The whole day focuses on our youth having direct contact with the Police Division in a way to help build better communications and better understanding," reported Valeisa George, the CHRC community relations specialist who developed the program with her husband, police officer Shawn George. "A lot of officers are out here; the fire department is out here. Their whole time is dedicated to making this day enjoyable for the youth."

The CHRC's second initiative in response to the riots was to introduce a nationally recognized program called Study Circles. "It is a grass-roots effort that will involve groups from all parts of the community in meetings at schools, congregations, businesses, and community organizations," the *Cincinnati Enquirer* reported in June 2001. Efforts were underway to bring the program to Cincinnati before the 2001 riots as a way to identify and reduce racial tension within the city. Lesley Jones, communications coordinator for the CHRC, said the commission "planned several types of programs over three to five years. The first year will focus on police-community relations, the second on race and the third on community building." According to a *Cincinnati Enquirer* article describing the implementation of the Study Circles, after a series of five meetings the results of the discussions would be ranked in order of importance and then turned over to Cincinnati Community Action Now for review and implementation. In a "To Whom It May Concern" letter dated May 28, 2002, Cecil Thomas reported on the results of the Greater Cincinnati Study Circles:

> The GCSC Program, organized by 13 citizen volunteers under the auspices of the CHRC, began face-to-face dialogue on improving community-police relations last year. Since the inception of the program, nearly 300 residents and 48 police officers have participated, and the Community-Police Partnership Task Force was formed because of those efforts. The Task Force, comprised of residents and police, has prioritized over 100 action ideas and selected one project to implement over

the summer. The project is a one-day event, a Community-Police Outreach Festival, to be held in various neighborhoods over the next 4–6 months. The Festivals are organized by the Task Force to include police and fire safety education, social service resources, job resources, and other service[s] to meet the needs of the homeless, low to moderate income households, youth, and the elderly in our community.

A third CHRC program, the Cincinnati Youth Streetworker Program (YSP), was started in the latter part of 2002 based on the Boston Gun Project, which used street workers to interact with youth. Thomas noted the program evolved into "what we have now as the Cincinnati Initiative to Reduce Violence . . . CIRV was designed as a result of Council's scream for how do we resolve all of the homicides in our city." The YSP used individuals who were former criminals to cooperate with police and work with 10 to 15 "clients" to change their lifestyles and reduce street violence. A report on the program published in 2003 described the effort as concentrating "resources, including youth programs and law enforcement, at the community level to improve safety and the quality of life for all community residents, including the hardest to serve population: youth on the street," in the Evanston, Madisonville, and Walnut Hills neighborhoods. "The program's target population," according to the report, "is individuals between the ages of 12 to 25, who reside in these targeted communities and who are 'street youth.' These individuals are typically economically disadvantaged, African-American, and unconnected with the needed resources to ensure success." The program was formally recognized by city council in 2007; although apparently successful, the program did not receive full funding from the council beyond 2009.

Under Thomas's leadership the CHRC flourished with several visible and successful programs and with renewed credibility as an effective agency for improving relations among Cincinnati's citizens, city agencies, and the police. An April 2003 *Cincinnati Enquirer* article commented on the CHRC's sixtieth anniversary: "Though it hasn't garnered much media attention, the Human Relations Commission has been a central player in trying to bring about citywide healing and improve the relationship between police and African-Americans." Thomas was quoted in the article saying: "Our function is to meet the needs of the citizens of Cincinnati. I think we've done that very effectively and that is why we've been around for 60 years." The article also provided a summary of the CHRC's activities and successes:

> The commission played a key role in helping resolve a dispute between African-American protestors and downtown restaurants that shut down during a black music festival in the summer of 2000. It helped to mobilize clergy, community leaders and other volunteers to walk the streets of Over-the-Rhine in an effort to keep peace during the April 2001 riots. The commission has played a part in helping to implement police reforms recommended by the U.S. Department of Justice. It has even been actively trying to bring city leaders and boycott organizers to the table to talk out an end to the 21-month-old boycott.
>
> The commission is probably best known, however, for intervening when police and citizens clash. Its 50 community relations monitors are routinely dispatched whenever there are public protests or police altercations with residents.

In 2005, Cecil Thomas resigned as executive director so that he could run for election to city council. In 2004, Thomas had secured a $75,000 grant from the Greater Cincinnati Foundation to fund the Youth Streetworker Program. When he approached city council for funding to continue the program, he was refused: "I was so distraught realizing the politics that come into play here that I said, 'I know how to fix this.' I'll step down as director and run for city council, that way I'll make sure that I get my support to keep the funding going. I stepped down on June 30, 2005, and I started my campaign to run for city council. I was elected and began my effort to make my changes." Thomas's efforts on council ultimately led to the formation of the Cincinnati Initiative to Reduce Violence in 2007. As a council member, Thomas was a firm supporter of the CHRC: "When I was a member of council, I would make sure folks understood the importance of the CHRC." Upon Thomas's resignation Lesley E. Jones, the CHRC's assistant director, was appointed acting director.

One of the best records of the CHRC's programs and activities in the community is found in a statement by Cecil Thomas. If one adds the Back on the Block and Community Relations Monitors programs to the list, the report reflects some of the useful work the CHRC has accomplished:

> I would be remiss if I did not recognize the dedicated staff and board of commissioners for their support. They have been a stabilizing force as we worked to address a number of issues that generated tension in our community. There have been many challenges and opportunities, but for the sake of brevity, I will only cite a few of the most notable here. CHRC mediated the racially charged misunderstanding between downtown restaurant owners and community members. CHRC served as bridge between citizens and police during the civil disturbances, and spent countless hours trying to find an agreeable common ground solution to the boycott. CHRC worked to preserve the peace on Fountain Square when the KKK came to town, and responded to a number of police-intervention shootings, providing a balanced perspective of what occurred. CHRC sponsored numerous community forums, including one meeting that received national attention in the aftermath of the Nathaniel Jones incident [the death of an African American man as the result of a fight with police]. CHRC worked with the Inter-Ethnic Council of Greater Cincinnati to mediate a misunderstanding between the Asian community and a potential developer for the city who allegedly voiced his lack of desire to rent to "Chinese." CHRC acted as a buffer between members of the Northside community and citizens who objected to a visible display of firearms during a neighborhood march. And finally, CHRC responded to the community of Price Hill to gather and disseminate to the public factual information relative to a wooden cross, found soaked in gasoline, in the yard of a black family, helping to quell rumors of a neighborhood engulfed in racial turmoil.

Norma Holt Davis, who had previously served as executive director of the Cincinnati chapter of the NAACP, was appointed to succeed Thomas as director of the CHRC in April 2006. Her term was short lived, as she soon resigned to campaign for a vacant county judgeship.

The commission moved quickly to fill the executive director position by appointing Cheryl Meadows to the post. Meadows, a longtime city hall insider, seemed a good choice after having served as assistant to the city manager and head of the Department of Neighborhood Services. Immediately before her CHRC appointment she had served for five years as city manager of Lincoln Heights, a predominately African American community north of Cincinnati. "I was asked to come because the agency was having problems with its contract with the city and meeting its objectives . . . I had previous experience in the city," said Meadows.

Despite Meadows's experience in city hall and Cecil Thomas's efforts as a member of city council, several council members reverted to form with questions about the need for the CHRC and proposals to cut its budget. "When I came in, it was about $365,000. But during my tenure there we took huge budget cuts. We had to cut people," Meadows said. The city council reduced the CHRC's budget to $155,000 for 2007. The council eventually restored funding for the Cincinnati Initiative to Reduce Violence but then separated the program from the CHRC. Some critics of the move felt it was done to allow some members of city council to take credit for any positive results from the CIRV efforts. Will Thomas, the CHRC board chair, wrote in a letter to council's budget committee, "It is with deep regret that we will need to cease operating, but the budget we received leaves us with no alternative." The $155,000 budget would provide salaries and benefits for five street workers and four staff members for one year. Will Thomas was quoted in the *Cincinnati Enquirer,* "When members of council don't understand what the agency does it becomes an easy target." CHRC street workers "put out fires and spike rumors," he said. Questions about the CHRC's budget and spending continued to be debated for several more months in 2007 before things seemed to quiet down and council members moved on to other issues.

Cheryl Meadows continued the CHRC's program and outreach efforts despite the agency's budget problems. The CHRC worked closely with the staff of the Ohio Civil Rights Commission and provided the organization with office space. The OCRC regional office was in Dayton, and Meadows wanted to be sure "they could be accessible to the people in Cincinnati." Even so, the persistent questions about the CHRC's value that had dogged the agency over its history continued to be raised. "It's a perennial question—what do they do?" Meadows lamented. She went on to say,

> We started a newsletter. We would go to community councils. We tried to reengage the agency in mediation. We would do everything we could to keep people informed. We would spotlight things that we were doing . . . you can get the [news]paper but do you read it? The question would always remain: "What do they do?" But you would always have one or two members who come to your defense. . . . I think the CHRC for a long time stayed around because politically it wouldn't look good not to fund the Human Relations Commission.

8

Completing Seventy

Years of Service

2010 to 2013

Polls noted in the British newspaper the Daily Mail *found that only about one-third of the persons surveyed believed race relations had improved in the two years President Barack Obama had been in office. On the legal front the Supreme Court ruled on cases involving voting districts and gay marriage.*

Incidents and racial tensions in local communities that had prevailed throughout the nation's history continued unabated. Violent encounters between African Americans and law enforcement officers continued in the early years of the decade. Although not the result of an encounter with police, the death of Trayvon Martin in Florida inflamed African Americans and set the stage for violent responses to the killings of other blacks over the following years. Protests and riots occurred in New York, Baltimore, Chicago, and Ferguson, Missouri, following deadly encounters between police officers and black citizens.

After serving five years in the position, Cheryl Meadows announced her retirement as executive director of the CHRC in January 2012. An article in the *Cincinnati Herald* listed important accomplishments during her tenure, including improved public awareness about the CHRC and its work, collaboration with the Ohio Civil Rights Commission and Housing Opportunities Made Equal, and policy changes in the city's hiring procedures for ex-offenders. The CHRC continued to play a role in the Cincinnati Initiative to Reduce Violence and Stop the Violence programs. As she retired, Meadows noted, the CHRC faced funding cuts: "despite our many accomplishments, the CHRC continues to face funding challenges. . . . The CHRC experienced a drastic reduction in 2011 in its funding from the city and subsequently had to eliminate staff and reduce staff salaries and benefits." CHRC staff member Juanita Bohannon was appointed acting director.

Dr. Ericka King-Betts, a graduate of Purdue University, was appointed executive director in August 2012. Dr. King-Betts had previously served as director of intervention and prevention programs for the Cincinnati YWCA. In a letter to the *Cincinnati Herald*, King-Betts listed the programs she was continuing to promote through her leadership of the CHRC.

> The Commission has broadened the scope of its advocacy to include police-community relations, youth empowerment, women's issues, and advocating for the disabled. The Commission has never lost its vision of embracing diversity and promotion of communal harmony. . . . A flagship and current program of the Commission is supplying Outreach Street Workers for the Cincinnati Initiative to Reduce Violence. CHRC also remains focused on being out in the community listening and working to help people overcome prejudice and discrimination and build mutual respect and understanding.

On November 16, 2013, the Cincinnati Human Relations Commission held a commemorative dinner to celebrate its seventieth anniversary. Looking toward the future, the agency that started in response to civil unrest during the Second World War pledged to meet its mission of building strong relations among the people of Cincinnati. In looking back over seventy years, it is obvious the agency's history has had, as *Cincinnati Enquirer* reporter Allen Howard wrote in 1986, "a rugged and controversial existence." Even so, it has persevered in promoting better human relations in Greater Cincinnati.

Conclusion

"A Rugged and Controversial Existence"

How then are we to assess the CHRC's "rugged and controversial existence"? The *Guidelines for Effective Human Relations Commissions*, promulgated in 2003 by the U.S. Department of Justice, are so general as to be of little use. The CHRC was fulfilling the DOJ's recommendations long before they were even formulated: employ a professional staff, involve local leadership, set goals, recommend policies, and develop programs; encourage minority employment and economic development; discourage prejudice and discrimination in the criminal justice system, business, and education.

But the question remains, how should the results of these activities be measured? Beyond a three-sentence call for a "Human Relations Report Card," the federal guidelines are silent on evaluation, and rightly so. The metrics of human relations success are nearly impossible to establish—how many opinions were changed, policies improved, stereotypes debunked, rights reinforced, riots averted? No one will ever know.

On a symbolic level, however, the CHRC's importance is evident. Embodying the city's commitment to civil and human rights, the agency has provided direct access to city hall for all minorities, a function not available through other community groups or organizations working for change.

On a programmatic level, the CHRC has, especially in recent decades, instituted a series of neighborhood-based activities—sometimes independently, at other times with cooperating agencies. Examples include the Cincinnati Initiative to Reduce Violence, the Summer Youth Employment Program, the Juvenile Accountability Block Grant, the Journeyman Union Manpower Program, Community Relations Monitors, the Youth Crime Prevention Project, the West End Community Adolescent Priority Project, Back on the Block (in collaboration with the Citizens Committee on Youth and the Cincinnati Recreation Commission), the Self-Help and Resource Exchange program, the Youth Ambassador Program, the Peace Bowl, the Great Youth Debate, Study Circles, and multiple strategies to improve police-community relations in collaboration with the Citizen's Review Board and the Cincinnati Police Department (the Police Division became the Police Department in late 2001). Some of these endeavors were short lived, some were much more successful than others, and some were simply the result of a nonprofit agency opportunistically chasing grant money to flesh out its budget. Nevertheless, many of these programs were established as a direct result of the CHRC's commitment to fulfill its mission to improve human relations.

Apart from the symbolic and practical work of the CHRC, some themes emerge from its history: municipal human relations agencies such as the CHRC played and continue to play an important role in the ongoing American civil rights movement; intergroup relations efforts in Cincinnati replicated a pattern that was typical nationwide; police-community relations and riot prevention will likely remain abiding elements of the municipal human relations agenda; and strong leaders were key actors at critical stages in the agency's development.

THE CHRC'S ROLE IN THE CIVIL RIGHTS MOVEMENT

The literature on the role of consensus-based, persuasion-oriented social-action organizations offers a basis for evaluating human relations efforts in Cincinnati. As sociologist Dennis Downey notes, agencies such as the CHRC can easily be dismissed as "movements of polite interest," "timid rebellions," or "disguised politics." After noting that these efforts "may have more modest, diffuse, and superficial consequences than movements of harsher texture," Downey goes on to point out:

Noncontentious activities can make important contributions to (social) movement development. Such activities are frequently designed not to produce social change directly, but to mobilize support or cultivate political opportunities for subsequent action to promote change. Their contributions are generally indirect and long-term, and cannot be accounted for in a narrow search for direct movement outcomes. As a consequence, such strategic choices are easily mistaken for timidity and/or naïveté.

Downey calls for a more sophisticated analysis, noting that this type of restraint is frequently used in concert with and, in fact, complements more aggressive strategies. Noncombative negotiations for social change in concert with direct-action tactics and grassroots mobilization form a kind of pincer maneuver that is difficult to deflect. From this perspective, social change often comes about when a more confrontational style is combined with a nonoppositional approach.

Municipal human relations agencies such as the CHRC give minority groups direct access to local government through internal advocacy, training, mediation, and persuasion. This is in clear contrast with the external actions (lawsuits, sit-ins, boycotts, marches) of nongovernmental organizations. When used together, internal and external pressures often result in improvements in human relations and in the recognition of civil rights. Marshall Bragdon, Cincinnati's pioneer human relations director, made this point quite succinctly:

> Political action at the state and national level promoted civil and voting rights, integrated education, and fair housing. In Cincinnati, local churches, the Urban League, and the NAACP led the efforts to integrate Coney Island and the Cincinnati Public Schools and to prevent police brutality. Working quietly to set the scene for social change, the MFRC and later the CHRC were certainly concerned but only marginally involved with these direct actions.

The narrative arc of the CHRC's history shows how it worked from within government in tandem with more combative external groups to achieve social change. Using a classic human relations approach, municipal agencies such as the CHRC are becoming an increasingly appreciated aspect of the civil rights movement.

THE CHRC AS A TYPICAL AGENCY

Rather than being exceptional, the CHRC is in many ways illustrative of its counterparts across the country during the latter part of the twentieth century and first decade of the twenty-first. In his essay "The Bureaucracy of Race," Burton Levy identifies the common attributes of municipal human relations agencies, many of which aptly characterize the CHRC:

- For the most part race relations dominated its agenda and continues to do so;

- It was significantly affected by the black power revolution of the 1960s, signifying a shift from gradualism to "immediatism" in its philosophy and programming;

- Believing they were goodwill ambassadors dedicated to resolving racial conflicts, its members did not perceive themselves as part of the problem;

- It was composed of elites representing various interest groups, causing the Commission to focus on issues of race, gender, gender identity, and ethnicity, for example, over those of social class;

- It experienced internal and external power shifts, struggles for power, conflicting personalities and ideologies, as well as faced the administrative problems and political effects of periodic reorganization;

- It worked with impressive mandates, minimal staffing, and inadequate funding;

- It had the typical combination of white director, black assistant director, and mostly white volunteers until the mid-1960s when hiring black professionals and recognizing minority leadership became a high priority;

- Its volunteer committee members and professional staff most often came from the religious, academic, legal, and nonprofit sectors, or other branches of government;

- It served as a springboard for the political careers of some former volunteers and professional staff members;

- It dealt with a fairly constant barrage of existential challenges from city administration, city council and department heads, as well as a variety of critics in the public and private sectors;

- It survived sharp criticism from both ends of the political and racial spectrum;

- In terms of programming, initial priorities were in the areas of housing, employment, police-community relations, and recreation. Over time, neighborhood engagement and a focus on youth were added;

- The increase in federal and state fair housing, equal employment, and civil rights laws (and their enforcement) narrowed its mission while creating a greater need for basic human relations work: education, communication, conciliation, mediation and facilitation.

Although most early municipal human relations agencies were founded in response to ethnic or racial disturbances (e.g., the Zoot Suit riots in Los Angeles or the Harlem riots in New York City), most evolved from crisis-motivated responses to riots into today's human relations councils and community commissions. Similar to the CHRC, many developed broader purviews that included, but were not limited to, race relations. Unlike the CHRC, however, some agencies obtained mandates to engage in enforcement activities, including issuing subpoenas and instituting criminal prosecutions. This was in addition to their basic functions such as operating bias and prejudice prevention programs and offering training for compliance with antidiscrimination laws.

After its transition from the MFRC in the mid-1960s, the CHRC became an incubator, developing leadership for other organizations across the city (e.g., Charles Judd at Housing Opportunities Made Equal; Susan Noonan at the Woman's City Club; Charles Hirt at People

Working Cooperatively; Michael Maloney at the Urban Appalachian Council), and sending human relations leaders to manage agencies in other cities (e.g., Eugene Sparrow to Grand Rapids; Marcia Hall-Craig to Fort Worth).

POLICE-COMMUNITY RELATIONS
AND RIOT PREVENTION

One aspect of the CHRC's past gives us a possible clue to its future. Throughout its seventy-year history the agency and the city it serves have consistently dealt with the drumbeat of police shootings and both real and perceived harassment of black citizens. This is not likely to change in the future. The Cincinnati Police Department is most active in low-income and working-class neighborhoods, where crimes are most frequently reported. These are also neighborhoods with many black residents. Stepped-up training and the trend toward using Tasers instead of guns may diminish the lethality of police-citizen encounters but will not reduce the tension inherent in many of these situations. The CHRC's two-pronged approach of training officers in human relations techniques along with working directly with minority youth in conflict avoidance will likely continue to be the centerpiece of its work.

Similar to other municipal intergroup-relations agencies, the roots of the CHRC lie in the paradoxical realm of riot prevention and response. Neither civil disturbances nor their underlying causes have been eliminated, as recent history in other cities has shown. The African American community has proven better able to articulate the causes of urban riots, and agencies sensitive to this information have been able at times to foresee, if not forestall, impending upheavals. An ongoing part of the CHRC's role may be to warn of rising levels of civic stress, to communicate the warning so clearly that the message is indeed heeded, and to recommend effective policies and programs to reduce that stress.

LEADERSHIP

The MFRC and the CHRC benefited from strong leaders who stood up at critical times. Among the agency's volunteers, several stand out, but of special note were Arthur Hull Jr., S. Arthur Spiegel, and Robert L. Black Jr. who, during their terms as board chairs during the pivotal

1960s, guided the agency through its transformation from the MFRC to the CHRC. Key roles were also played by the agency's directors. Four in particular are emblematic of effective leadership during their respective eras: Marshall Bragdon, Virginia Coffey, Arzell Nelson, and Cecil Thomas.

Marshall Bragdon was a pioneer in the mid-twentieth-century municipal human relations movement, both locally with the Mayor's Friendly Relations Commission and nationally as a founder and president of the National Association of Intergroup Relations Officials. As executive director of the MFRC he orchestrated subtle, behind-the-scenes negotiations for racial conciliation. In addition to the committee members who themselves constituted an elite cadre of volunteers, his constituency was the mayor, city council, the heads of city departments, and the leadership of unions, media outlets, businesses, schools, and hospitals, the majority of whom were white. He cooperated with the heads of minority organizations but mainly dealt with the enforcers of the status quo, which gave the appearance of serving the status quo—what some critics called "the rightness of whiteness." Bragdon's role was neither sinister nor atypical for the times, simply reflective of how human relations were conducted in the 1940s and 1950s. In 1950 the *Cincinnati Post and Times Star* said of the MFRC, "'Cincinnati's 11-Foot Pole' is the tag attached to the [M]ayors Friendly Relations Committee because it handles situations most people wouldn't touch with a 10-foot pole." Bragdon wielded that "11-foot pole" with the tenacity and diplomacy required by the social conditions of the time.

Fifteen years later the same newspaper would sum up the agency's work succinctly and accurately: "Through less-than-dramatic action the committee worked behind the scenes to ease community tensions and expand the human rights of all residents of Cincinnati." The gains the MFRC made on behalf of racial progress in Cincinnati, while frustratingly small, were nonetheless valuable. Under Bragdon's guidance the MFRC worked what might be called the quiet side of the civil rights movement.

Marshall Bragdon's two-decade tenure at the MFRC was matched by Virginia Coffey's service to both the MFRC and the CHRC. Coffey was not only a bridge between the two, she represented a nationwide inflection point between two eras in human relations work. She expanded the purview of the CHRC to include not only affective action (persuasion, mediation, education) but also effective action (programs involving youth, neighborhoods, minority communities). She set a proactive tone for the CHRC by enabling urban Appalachians to establish their own advocacy organization, a precedent that would be followed by subsequent directors working to empower women, Hispanics, former felons, people with disabilities, and members of the LGBTQ community. "Based on her work in the West End before joining the MFRC and her experience in the East End and Over-the-Rhine afterwards, Virginia Coffey (and her successors) shepherded the CHRC toward an expansion of the city's human relations focus from research, education, and arbitration to encompass neighborhood engagement and minority empowerment."

Arzell Nelson's nearly three decades of staff experience culminated in his six-year term as executive director. In that capacity he provided stability to the agency's administration and kept it free of political entanglements at city hall. His background with effective CHRC programs such as Back on the Block and the Community Relations Monitors ensured their ongoing success. Nelson also mentored other leaders, particularly Susan Noonan, who served as acting director for two years after his retirement.

From 2000 through 2005, Cecil Thomas deftly handled both internal and external crises as the CHRC's executive director. He stepped into that position even as city council threatened to dismantle the agency and parcel out its programs to other organizations; he deflected that internal threat while bolstering the agency's police-community relations and youth programming. Thomas had been director only a year before a police officer killed an unarmed black youth in Over-the-Rhine, causing several days of violent disorder.

Thomas spent time on the streets to get a feel for needed programs, then went into action developing "A Day in the Park" with the Cincinnati Police Department, launching the local Study Circles program, and writing grants for the Cincinnati Streetworkers program, which evolved into the Cincinnati Initiative to Reduce Violence. Throughout it all he worked for large-scale police reforms and to end the boycott of Cincinnati by national black organizations. When he resigned from CHRC to run for city council, in June 2005, he remained a staunch advocate for the agency, especially in budget negotiations. By fighting to save the agency, responding to a serious civil disturbance, and developing an administrative structure and effective programs to address the issues stressing intergroup relations in the city, Cecil Thomas fully represented the new era in human-relations work introduced by Virginia Coffey.

Returning to the question of how to assess the CHRC's "rugged and controversial existence," the words of Lewis Clingman, an academic historian who also chaired a human relations commission in Michigan, provide an apt appraisal of the CHRC's first seven decades: "To conclude the Human Relations Commission was a total failure would be neither just nor honest; to consider it an unqualified success would be imprudent and false. Like so many intergroup agencies, the Commission did its task as it understood the task at the time. . . . Truly it was another 'noble experiment.'"

Epilogue

In late 2015, intergroup relations in Cincinnati entered a new phase with the adoption of recommendations first made in 1965. The city council voted to amend the ordinance that established the Cincinnati Human Relations Commission, moving the functions of the CHRC from the Department of Community and Economic Development to a new Office of Human Relations (OHR). This new entity is to be administered by "a human relations manager appointed by and under the supervision of the city manager." Some members of the OHR staff will become city employees, qualifying for Civil Service benefits and, although the CHRC may continue to exist as a 501(c)(3) tax-exempt organization solely for the purposes of receiving grants and donations, a new advisory board will be established.

The Office of Human Relations is charged with

> the investigation and review of complaints against the City or its independent boards and commissions of alleged discrimination in services, employment practices or personnel policies based on race, gender, age, color, religion, disability status, marital status, sexual orientation or transgender status, or ethnic, national or Appalachian region; the review of compliance with non-discrimination provisions of City contracts by contractors doing business with the City or its independent boards

and commissions; and the investigation of complaints regarding the impact of relocation of neighborhood residents and urban development on the City's diverse population.

In addition, current programming will remain in place.

Appendix A

MFRC/CHRC Timeline

1943

- Cincinnati city council passes resolution forming Friendly Relations Committee.

- Office space in city hall is designated for MFRC use; Martha Ong is appointed temporary executive, assisted by "Negro stenographer."

1944

- First meeting of MFRC general committee is held; Robert Segal of Jewish Community Council is appointed secretary.

- MFRC operates on $100 donation.

- MFRC takes no action when crowd of 50 to 100 people stones two black families' homes in Mt. Adams because they are "first Negro residents" on the street.

- MFRC hopes to avoid postwar "employment discrimination" by studying local companies with integration programs and produces pamphlet, *They Do Work Together,* the following year.

- MFRC sponsors first Friendly Relations Week, promoting tolerance, including an Institute on Propaganda, Housing, and Jobs to address problems faced by blacks in particular.

- Paul Robeson is honored at MFRC-sponsored luncheon.

1945

- Marshall Bragdon is appointed executive director.

- MFRC adopts a constitution.

- First issue of MFRC newsletter, *Building Together,* is published.

- City manager appropriates $10,000 for MFRC's annual budget.

- MFRC shares office space with newly formed Police Division Race Relations Detail.

- Recommendation is made to public schools' Board of Athletics and University of Cincinnati (UC) Athletic Department that no games be scheduled "which would prevent Negro athletes from playing." Public schools comply; UC says it will cooperate "where possible."

- MFRC assists with resettlement of Japanese Americans after wartime internment.

- Bragdon is appointed "impartial conciliator" between restaurant operators and those protesting discrimination against black patrons.

1946

- MFRC works to defuse racial tensions after alleged black rape of white woman in West End; notes "injudicious and hysterical" reporting by local newspapers and radio stations.

- On behalf of MFRC, Bragdon mediates between two discriminatory employers and black job seekers, gaining one black hire by each employer.

- MFRC and Division of Negro Welfare intervene in dispute between white and black high school students.

- At city budget hearings "spokesmen for real estate and taxpayer groups demand MFRC's demise as a needless 'frill.'"

- City manager appropriates $12,000 for MFRC's annual budgets for 1946, 1947, and 1948.

- MFRC participates in ongoing efforts to integrate Cincinnati Bar Association, Coney Island, local movie theaters, restaurants, roller rinks, bowling alleys, and physician staffs of local hospitals.

- MFRC sponsors Let's All Be Friendly Week.

1947

- MFRC begins scholarship for public school teachers to attend summer workshops in intercultural education.

- MFRC acknowledges cases of police brutality as "our most publicized headache" yet refuses to join Council of Churches, NAACP, Woman's City Club, Jewish Community Relations Council, and West End Civic League in signing joint letter protesting a particular case of police brutality.

- MFRC sponsors a single "race relations" talk given to rookie police officers by New York University psychology professor.

- MFRC opens borrowing library of over 1,000 books, pamphlets, and literature on intergroup relations.

1948

- MFRC works with public library's Films and Recordings division to build up inventory of resources on intergroup relations; encourages local theaters to screen films such as *Don't Be a Sucker*, *Crossfire*, and *Gentlemen's Agreement*.

- MFRC sponsors local stop of Freedom Train, intended to promote citizenship by displaying important historical documents.

- MFRC works with radio stations WLW and WSAI to air programming on intergroup relations.

- MFRC works with Girl Scouts to establish interracial day camps.

- MFRC helps coordinate conversion of Council of Social Agencies' Division of Negro Welfare into Cincinnati branch of

Urban League; donates $1,500 in discretionary funding to new
Urban League office.

- West Virginia native Virginia Coffey hired as assistant executive
secretary of MFRC; Coffey begins regular column in local newspapers featuring the work of MFRC.

1949

- Because many standing committees are not functioning and
many members of general committee are not actively involved,
MFRC reorganizes its committee and membership structures.

- Informal evaluation of MFRC's first five years shows little
progress made in civil rights, police-community relations, public
relations (e.g., establishing speaker's bureau), countering anti-
Semitism, or in integrating employment, housing, health care,
recreational facilities.

- Two new city council members challenge MFRC's budget request and question its effectiveness; evidence of broad community support for MFRC is sent to council's finance committee.

- MFRC incorporates as nonprofit corporation and receives
$15,000 lump sum payment from city to perform "certain spe-
cific services for the city."

1950

- MFRC mediates between protesters and city over fatal police
shooting in Walnut Hills.

- MFRC successfully works to initiate integration of swimming
pools operated by Public Recreation Commission; also works
with Board of Education to facilitate desegregation of high
school swimming pools.

- MFRC counters "cheap exploitation of racial prejudice" by
local union using black members to force a restaurant to unionize its workforce.

- MFRC assists with integration of city's water meter readers.

1951

- After continual urging by MFRC, Conservatory of Music and College of Music agree to admit blacks; MFRC returns to issue of desegregating Coney Island, but with little effect.

- Marshall Bragdon is invited to address police recruit classes on intergroup relations.

- Virginia Coffey entertains international delegation from World Youth Assembly at home, responds to visitors' hard questions about discriminatory treatment of Africans in the group.

- Dorothy Dolbey becomes first woman to serve as MFRC's chair.

1952

- City council tasks MFRC to study "discrimination in employment and fair employment practices in Cincinnati."

- MFRC initiates program of annual briefings for Protestant clergy on "racial, religious, and cultural problems and progress."

- MFRC turns attention to lack of black firefighters in Cincinnati after qualified black applicant is rejected on technicality.

- MFRC continues to work on segregation issue at Coney Island as it becomes more contentious.

- MFRC monitors vocal opposition to building new public housing in Northside.

1953

- MFRC issues results of year-long study of local employment practices in "Report Concerning Racial Discrimination in Employment in the Cincinnati Area" and recommends Fair Employment Practices Ordinance be passed by city council; council fails to pass the ordinance.

- MFRC examines blockbusting tactics used by realtors in Avondale.

- MFRC continues to work with schools through human relations workshops.

- MFRC continues to work on desegregating of Coney Island, but with little effect.

- MFRC successfully urges Civil Service Commission to collect data on race *after* employment, not before.

- MFRC hosts conference on placing open-occupancy clause in municipal contract to sell water to Forest Park; clause is not included in contract.

1954

- MFRC sees positive support for its position on desegregation in Brown v. Board of Education.

- MFRC is vindicated by partial desegregation of Coney Island.

- MFRC addresses unrest in West End over police activity with investigative report, a meeting bringing West End residents to the table, and stepping up human relations training for all ranks of police officers.

- MFRC urges calm as black homeowners move into Evanston.

- MFRC prints and circulates *Mission to the Mountaineer,* based on pastor's ministry to Appalachians in Walnut Hills.

- MFRC discusses Appalachian migrant work at first UC Workshop on Intergroup Relations.

- Despite MFRC training efforts, 15-year-old black student is shot by police.

- MFRC monitors impact of urban renewal and expressway projects on black housing stock.

- MFRC sponsors Workshop on the Southern Mountaineer in Cincinnati, and followed up by 50-page printed report circulated widely.

- MFRC prints and distributes speech about Appalachian migrants by Dr. Roscoe Giffin at National Federation of Settlements conference.

- Marshall Bragdon completes term as president of National Association of Intergroup Relations Officials.

1955

- City manager requests MFRC investigate and report on "police methods" during incidents in West End.

- MFRC organizes "regular conferences" between police and community members.

- Police Division requests MFRC conduct community relations and intergroup communications for police officers.

1956

- Consultation is provided to pastors in Evanston to ease tensions because African Americans are moving into the community.

- MFRC offers assistance and support to Rev. Michael Hamilton, Episcopal priest who is beginning a service for "mountaineers."

- MFRC receives numerous inquiries from all parts of the country seeking information about the Southern migrant workshop.

- Roscoe Giffin conducts 25 interviews with migrant men, women, and children with aid of MFRC's Janet Smith.

- MFRC reprints and distributes 1,000 copies of Giffin's article "From Cinder Hollow to Cincinnati," published in *Mountain Life and Work* in the fall.

- MFRC releases third printing of 1,000 copies of report on Giffin's 1954 workshop.

1957

- Citizens Committee on Youth is established as contractual agency in the mold of MFRC.

- City council fails to pass Fair Employment Ordinance first proposed by MFRC in 1953.

- *Cincinnati Enquirer* reporter William Collins consults MFRC for seven-part series on Appalachian migrants to Cincinnati.

- MFRC reaches out to American Indians relocated to Cincinnati but fails to connect.

- After fatal police shooting of 14-year-old black male, MFRC is subject to "sharp criticism and hostility;" MFRC responds with defensive memo.

- MFRC serves as clearinghouse for information and questions related to migrants in support of Ford Foundation grant to Berea College to fund an Appalachian regional study.

1958

- MFRC distributes copies of "Ministry to the Southern Mountaineer," report prepared by The Rev. Michael Hamilton, an Episcopal priest.

- Mayor requests that Marshall Bragdon review charges by NAACP about recent police incidents including shooting death of young man; as a result of review, MFRC board adopts policy statement of agency's proper role in these matters.

1959

- After seven years of unsuccessful efforts by MFRC at local level, State of Ohio passes Fair Employment Practices law.

- Richard Guggenheim of MFRC board is appointed chair of new Ohio Civil Rights Commission.

- MFRC collaborates with Berea College to establish first Appalachian Workshop for teachers, civil servants, social workers, etc.

- As racial tensions grow over housing, MFRC's Committee on Changing Neighborhoods studies eight "change areas," to little effect.

- MFRC works with local newspaper editors to lessen racial identification in crime reporting.

1960

- Marshall Bragdon writes that what MFRC accomplished between 1943 and 1960 "seems now rather ineffectual."

- Edward Becker resigns from Cincinnati Public Schools board, believing he was denied its presidency because of his race; MFRC declines to comment.

- Deaths of two black youth at hands of police result in calls for city council to set up police review board; MFRC "did not support or oppose the review board."

- NAACP pickets local Woolworth stores to protest discrimination in service and employment; MFRC suggests it's an issue for Ohio Civil Rights Commission.

- MFRC's Virginia Coffey chairs National Association of Intergroup Relations Officials annual meeting in Cincinnati.

1961

- Basin Area Strategy Committee is formed with assistance of MFRC.

- MFRC endorses Dr. James Conant's position that black youth aged 16 to 21 are "social dynamite."

- Ohio passes Public Accommodations Law, opening all sections of Coney Island to everyone.

- Virginia Coffey is criticized for handling complaint against police officer who was at first disciplined, then cleared of charges.

- Virginia Coffey consults in Britain on "rising colour problem" there.

- MFRC starts informal potluck meetings featuring speakers and discussion on current human relations topics.

- Louise Spiegel joins MFRC as volunteer aide to make fact-finding field trips and help Berea workshop alumni remain active.

- MFRC joins Council of the Southern Mountains' Hands-across-the-Ohio program.

1962

- Virginia Coffey leaves MFRC after 14½ years of service to work at Seven Hills Neighborhood Houses; Eugene Sparrow is named new assistant director of MFRC.

- MFRC addresses racial references in newspaper real estate ads, segregated Cincinnati Real Estate Board, and neighborhoods closed to black home buyers; two proposed city ordinances, including one endorsed by MFRC, aimed at rectifying these problems fail to pass.

1963

- Mobilization for civil rights in the South prompts complaints in Cincinnati about use of police dogs, lack of blacks on city boards and commissions, and an all-white city council; this causes MFRC to reevaluate "its functions and format, in relation to present demands, and proposed changes."

- MFRC steps up work with local churches on desegregating neighborhoods and housing.

- MFRC and NAACP cooperate on increasing construction jobs for black workers.

- Cincinnati city council begins discussions of establishing Human Relations Commission based on MFRC's year-long self-evaluation.

- While NAACP notes, "the Negro community has very little regard for the MFRC," MFRC works with NAACP to establish police-citizen committee.

- MFRC and Council of the Southern Mountains cosponsor two-day Institute on Appalachian Migrants attended by 375 participants.

1964

- Process is underway to review and restructure Mayor's Friendly Relations Committee and rename it Cincinnati Human Relations Commission.

- MFRC works as mediator between Cincinnati Public Schools, NAACP, and CORE to end school boycott.

- MFRC establishes Community Relations Consultant Committee to work with Cincinnati Public Schools.

- MFRC works with several neighborhoods on housing discrimination issues.

1965

- Marshall Bragdon resigns as executive director.

- Eugene Sparrow is appointed acting executive director.

- MFRC is reorganized into nonprofit commission known as Cincinnati Human Relations Commission (CHRC).

1966

- David D. McPheeters is appointed executive director.

1967

- McPheeters resigns as executive director.

- Clinton L. Reynolds is appointed acting executive director.

- Staff and commissioners work to alleviate turmoil of June 12 riot following disputed conviction of Posteal Laskey Jr.

1968

- CHRC goes through administrative disarray and two executive directors in two years; Mayor Eugene Ruehlmann reaches out to newly formed human rights group, Metropolitan Area Religious Coalition of Cincinnati.

- Virginia Coffey is appointed (first female) executive director.

- Housing Opportunities Made Equal (HOME) is incorporated as nonprofit organization.

1969

- Coffey is selected as *Cincinnati Enquirer* Woman of the Year.

- CHRC creates new Community Relations Division.

- CHRC serves as consultant to Model Cities program staff.

- CHRC publishes 1969 Survey of City Employment for Mayor's Task Force on Employment.

1970

- CHRC creates advisory committee to work with Cincinnati Public Schools.

- Appalachian Fund provides financial support for student summer intern.

- CHRC cosponsors with Catholic Commission on Human Relations workshop on communication skills for community councils.

- Cosponsors second Xavier University Conference on Southern Appalachians in Cincinnati, which leads to formation of Appalachian Committee.

- Office of Urban Commitment is merged with CHRC.

- CHRC provides support for first Appalachian Festival sponsored by Junior League of Cincinnati.

1971

- Virginia Coffey leads reorganization of National Association of Intergroup Relations Officials to establish National Association of Human Rights Workers.

- Pilot project with Xavier University and University of Cincinnati to assign student teachers to work with individual students in their neighborhoods.

- Tension Alert Committee is established to alleviate racial tension on local college campuses and high schools.

- New police chief appoints CHRC Law Division members as his Community Advisory Board.

- CHRC publishes report that leads to revision of Police Division firearms policy.

1972

- Mayor declares January Cincinnati's Human Relations Month.

- Virginia Coffey announces CHRC appointment of Michael Maloney as Research and Appalachian Specialist, a position partially funded by Appalachian Fund.

- Appalachian Committee is formally established by CHRC.

- CHRC helps fund an office for Appalachian Committee in Railway Clerks Building.

1973

- Mayor declares week of November 11 Human Relations Week.

- CHRC helps Junior League of Cincinnati form Appalachian Community Development Association to sponsor annual Appalachian Festival.

1974

- Virginia Coffey resigns as executive director.
- Thomas L. Garner is appointed executive director.
- CHRC helps establish Urban Appalachian Council and dissolves Appalachian Committee.
- CHRC publishes first *The Social Areas of Cincinnati: Toward an Analysis of Needs* by staff member Michael E. Maloney. Based on census data, it later becomes useful planning tool for area non-profit organizations.

1975

- CHRC joins committee to form Martin Luther King Jr. Coalition and plans annual event celebrating Martin Luther King Day.
- CHRC manages affirmative action training program for city employees.
- CHRC collaborates with HUD to sponsor conference on housing.
- CHRC participates in Urban Corps program.
- CHRC creates Neighborhood Register of community-based organizations.

1976

- CHRC receives federal grant for Student Concerns Project to address racial issues in several high schools.

- CHRC creates Affirmative Marketing Program in Housing with Community Development funding.

- CHRC establishes Committee for Women.

- CHRC establishes program in cooperation with Police Division for CHRC staff to "ride-along" with police officers.

- CHRC serves as liaison between American Indian activist traveling through Cincinnati and city organizations and agencies.

- CHRC Housing Division issues report about neighborhood "red-lining" practices by realtors and banks.

- Urban Appalachian Council is recognized as independent agency with three-year contract with CHRC.

1977

- CHRC Community Relations staff is asked to work with Police Division in crowd control at Riverfront Stadium events.

- Police ride-along program is extended to CHRC board members.

- Student Concerns Project is continued and extended to include Mt. Healthy School District.

- CHRC collaborates with Housing Opportunities Made Equal in Fair Housing Program.

- CHRC cosponsors Emergency Housing Conference.

1978

- CHRC drafts and submits Fair Housing Ordinance to city council for consideration.

- At CHRC's request U.S. Commission on Civil Rights agrees to investigate city's procedures regarding complaints about police use of excessive force.

- CHRC forms Cincinnati area Human Rights Coalition, including numerous local organizations to address common concerns about civil rights issues.

1979

- City council establishes Office of Municipal Investigations (OMI) to investigate and resolve citizen complaints about police officers and other city personnel; CHRC's responsibility for investigations is transferred to OMI.
- U.S. Commission on Civil Rights conducts hearings on relationship between citizens and Police Division, at request of CHRC.
- CHRC issues studies of public service employee layoffs and gathers information for Cincinnati Coalition for People with Disabilities.

1980

- CHRC organizes Education Town Meeting to discuss issues and future direction of education in Cincinnati.
- CHRC issues preliminary report on Potential for Civil Disorder in Cincinnati.
- Memorial fund is established for prevention of youth violence.

1981

- Mayor declares Year of the Citizen.
- CHRC works with Police Division to address areas of tension, including interracial youth incidents and a cross burning.
- Women's Equality Day is held on Fountain Square, August 25.
- Opportunity Day is initiated to promote understanding of disabilities.

1982

- Thomas Garner resigns as executive director.

- Marcia Hall-Craig is appointed acting director.

- CHRC implements Advanced Crisis Control Techniques training program for members of Police Division.

- CHRC begins summer intern program for college students to work in high-tension communities.

- CHRC publishes Black Diversity and Neighborhood Registry documents.

1983

- Marcia Hall-Craig is promoted to executive director.

- CHRC sponsors film series in schools about human relations.

- CHRC organizes and conducts Training Symposium on Institutional Racism and Discrimination and Major Disabilities.

- CHRC prepares and distributes police-community relations brochure.

- CHRC and Police Division implement student ride-along program.

1984

- Marcia Hall-Craig resigns as executive director.

- Hilda M. Coaston is appointed acting director.

- George J. Penn is appointed executive director.

- CHRC establishes Ethelrie Harper Award, in recognition of individuals who demonstrate leadership in promoting positive human relations.

- CHRC's first annual Human Relations Conference is held.

1985

- "Attitudes about Cincinnati and Intergroup Relations" survey and report is issued.

- Second *Social Areas of Cincinnati* is published by CHRC. Future editions are produced by UC School of Planning.

1986

- George Penn resigns as executive director.

- Dr. W. Monty Whitney is appointed executive director.

- CHRC sponsors Cincinnati Black and Jewish Youth Experience.

- CHRC participates in organizing Black Family Coalition year-long activities.

- At request of city manager, CHRC studies city employment opportunities and issues "Report on Minority Advancement Opportunities in the City of Cincinnati."

- CHRC receives second-place Community Partnership Prize from National Organization on Disabilities.

1987

- CHRC initiates Youth Crime Prevention Project.

- CHRC receives Open Door Award from Greater Cincinnati Coalition of People with Disabilities.

1988

- CHRC initiates West End Community Adolescent Priorities Project (WECAPP), modeled after Youth Crime Prevention Project.

- CHRC establishes Disabled Affairs Committee.

- CHRC initiates Project Cool, collaborative effort with several agencies and organizations to assist residents during intense summer heat wave.

1989

- CHRC begins working with Housing Opportunities Made Equal to bring about compliance with Fair Housing Act.
- Juneteenth Celebration is instituted as annual event celebrating end of slavery.

1990

- CHRC assists in development of Operation Street Corner hotline and block watch programs in Laurel Homes community.
- Funding is received to continue West End Community Adolescent Project and Youth Crime Intervention Project.

1991

- CHRC initiates its summer Back on the Block program.
- CHRC sponsors Everybody Counts workshops for Cincinnati Public Schools students.
- Community Oriented Policing teams pair CHRC staff and police officers to walk in neighborhoods.

1992

- Dr. Monty Whitney resigns as executive director.
- Arzell Nelson is appointed executive director.
- CHRC begins Community Relations Monitors Program.

- CHRC organizes and conducts How to Handle Conflict workshops.
- CHRC holds Forum on Poverty for community leaders.

1993

- CHRC begins Celebrate Friendship Campaign in response to Ku Klux Klan symbol on Fountain Square.
- CHRC assists in facilitating Resident Advisory Board for Cincinnati Metropolitan Housing Authority residents to resolve issues from grassroots perspective.

1994

- CHRC begins Educational Luncheon series.
- Self-Help and Resources Exchange food program is initiated.

1995

- CHRC establishes Inter-Ethnic Council, an organization of 28 ethnic groups.
- CHRC produces 33 *InFocus* TV programs aired on CitiCable.
- CHRC sponsors workshop on Valuing and Managing Diversity in the Workplace.
- CHRC sponsors Cincinnati Human Relations Luncheon Series speakers.
- CHRC counters Ku Klux Klan activities through Celebrate Friendship campaign and planting Friendship Grove of trees in Eden Park.

1996

- Cincinnati Reds host Celebrate Diversity day at July game and provide 10,000 tickets for CHRC to distribute.

- CHRC conducts two public hearings on Hate Crimes/Ethnic Intimidation and Sexual Orientation.

- CHRC holds three Youth Empowerment Forums.

- CHRC establishes archives by sending 49 boxes of files to UC Library Archives and Rare Books collection.

- CHRC participates in international Talking Stones project by honoring former executive directors Marshall Bragdon and Virginia Coffey.

1997

- CHRC collaborates with several Cincinnati organizations and corporations to sponsor Jackie Robinson Day to commemorate famed baseball player's first appearance at the plate in Cincinnati.

- CHRC helps establish Chuck Harmon Youth Baseball Fund to recognize first African American Cincinnati Reds player and to support youth baseball in Cincinnati's inner-city neighborhoods.

1998

- Arzell Nelson resigns as executive director.

- Susan Noonan is appointed acting director.

- CHRC coordinates volunteer efforts for city's first Ujima CinciBration.

- CHRC community relations monitors work to decrease tension in Northside after a homicide.

1999

- City council commissions study on effectiveness of CHRC; study recommends city contract with independent, nonprofit corporation to provide some services.

- CHRC receives recognition from Blacks in Government.

- CHRC assists Pull Together Movement group in bringing UniverSoul Circus to Cincinnati.

2000

- Cecil Thomas is appointed acting director, then executive director.

- City council study commissioned in 1999 critical of CHRC is released to public in January.

2001

- Riots follow shooting death of Timothy Thomas by Cincinnati police officer.

- CHRC's Study Circles program is initiated to foster discussion about community-police relations following riots.

- CHRC and Police Division sponsor A Day in the Park community programs for over 3,000 youth.

2002

- CHRC signs Friends of the Collaborative agreement in response to Timothy Thomas shooting.

- Youth Streetworker Program is initiated based on Boston Gun Project.

2003

- CHRC expands Study Circles program and holds Community Outreach Festivals in all five police districts.

- *InFocus* programs are aired on commercial TV station WXIX.

- CHRC produces video created and performed by community youth titled "Do It Right."

- CHRC establishes Unity Ambassadors program for youth to assist in hosting events.

2004

- CHRC is active in leadership efforts to repeal city ordinance commonly referred to as Equal Rights, Not Special Rights, which restricted rights of gay and lesbian citizens.

- CHRC implements Unity Ambassadors program for youth.

- CHRC sponsors Solution 2004 Youth Forum at Xavier University.

2005

- Cecil Thomas resigns as executive director.

- Lesley E. Jones appointed acting director.

- CHRC develops Youth Ambassadors program.

2006

- Norma Holt Davis is appointed executive director and soon resigns position.

- Cheryl Meadows is appointed executive director.

- National Underground Railroad Freedom Center, opened in Cincinnati in 2002, recognizes CHRC as Freedom Station partner.

2007

- Cincinnati Initiative to Reduce Violence (CIRV) is formed.

- CHRC begins Summer Youth Employment Program.
- CHRC holds first Peace Bowl.

2008

- CHRC celebrates 65th anniversary.
- CHRC and other organizations respond to insults against people of Islamic faith.
- CHRC cosponsors community forum at National Underground Railroad Freedom Center for people of faith to discuss reconciling differences.
- CHRC outreach staff helps ex-offenders.

2009

- Ohio Civil Rights Commission office moves to CHRC office.
- CHRC hosts delegation from Bangladesh.
- CHRC promotes peace between at-risk youth at 3rd Annual Peace Bowl.
- CIRV works with Police Department to provide violence reduction resources at resource fairs in three neighborhoods.

2010

- CHRC hosts summit on mass incarceration.
- With Hamilton County Developmental Disabilities Services, CHRC sponsors PhotoVoice project with mentees and mentors.
- Human Relations Summit focuses on Cincinnati's African American community.
- CHRC uses CitiCable program to focus on hate crimes, inclusion, hunger, and Gay Chamber of Commerce.

2011

- CIRV Street Advocates team restored to full funding.

- CHRC and Urban League continue cooperation on summer youth employment projects with human relations focus.

- CHRC partners with League of United Latin American Citizens to bring their national convention to Cincinnati.

2012

- Cheryl Meadows resigns as executive director.

- Juanita Howard-Bohanan appointed acting director.

- Dr. Ericka King-Betts appointed executive director.

- CHRC renews focus on youth programming and complaint investigation.

- CHRC strengthens relationships with affiliated programs such as YWCA, Ohio Civil Rights Commission, Community Action Agency, and Housing Opportunities Made Equal.

2013

- CHRC renews emphasis on mediation and intervention services.

- CHRC hosts Midwest conference of human rights organizations.

- CHRC expands CIRV program to include street outreach workers.

- CHRC: Celebrating 70 Years as the Voice of the Community luncheon and anniversary dinner dance are held.

Appendix B

Chairs and Directors

CHAIRS OF THE MAYOR'S FRIENDLY RELATIONS COMMITTEE, 1943–64

Dr. Claude V. Courter	1943–46
Paul Steer	1947–48
Karl T. Finn	1949–50
Mrs. James (Dorothy N.) Dolbey	1951
Vincent H. Beckman Jr.	1952
Simon Lazarus Jr.	1953–54
Charles M. Judd	1955–56
Dr. Carter V. Good	1957–58
Leonard D. Slutz	1959–60
Arthur F. Hull Jr.	1961–62
Joseph L. Leinwohl	1963–64

CHAIRS OF THE CINCINNATI HUMAN RELATIONS COMMISSION, 1965–2013

S. Arthur Spiegel	1965–66
Robert L. Black Jr.	1967–69
Smith H. Tyler Jr.	1970–71
Robert R. Fitzpatrick Jr.	1972–73
Dr. John L. Henderson	1974–76
Mrs. Alvin (Ann) Bunis	1976–77
Bernard L. Rosenberg	1977–79
Donald J. Mooney Jr.	1979–80
Rev. James E. Milton	1980–83

Mark A. Vander Laan	1984–85
Richard A. Weiland	1986–88
Vincent B. Stamp	1989–90
William M. Spillers	1991–92
David Lazarus	1993–94
Rev. Damon Lynch III	1995–96
Michael W. Hawkins	1996–97
Gwen L. Robinson	1998
Ernest J. Waits Jr.	1998–2001
Dr. Arthur Shriberg	2002–4
Will Thomas	2005–7
George Wharton	2007–8
Karen Dabdoub	2009–10
Robert L. Harris	2011–13

EXECUTIVE DIRECTORS OF THE MAYOR'S FRIENDLY RELATIONS COMMITTEE, 1943–65

Martha Ong (acting)	1943–45
Marshall Bragdon	1945–65

EXECUTIVE DIRECTORS OF THE CINCINNATI HUMAN RELATIONS COMMISSION, 1966–2013

Eugene Sparrow (acting)	1965–66
David D. McPheeters	1966–67
Clinton L. Reynolds (acting)	1967–68
Virginia Coffey	1968–73
Thomas L. Garner	1974–82
Marcia Hall-Craig (acting)	1982–83
Marcia Hall-Craig	1983–84
Hilda M. Coaston (acting)	1984
George J. Penn	1984–85
Dr. W. Monty Whitney	1986–92
Arzell Nelson	1992–98
Susan Noonan (acting)	1998–2000
Cecil Thomas (acting)	2000

CHAIRS AND DIRECTORS

Cecil Thomas	2000–2005
Lesley E. Jones (acting)	2005–6
Norma Holt Davis	2006
Cheryl R. Meadows	2007–12
Juanita Howard-Bohannon (acting)	2012
Dr. Ericka King-Betts	2013

Sources

The following frequently cited sources are abbreviated in the references.

ARBA   Cincinnati Human Relations Commission Records, Archives and Rare Books Library, University of Cincinnati, US-15-01.

ARBB   Cincinnati Human Relations Commission Records, Archives and Rare Books Library, University of Cincinnati, S 32.His1.

ARBS   Judge S. Arthur Spiegel Papers, Archives and Rare Books Library, University of Cincinnati.

CHL   Virginia Coffey Papers, 1935–1984, Cincinnati History Library and Archives.

CHLU   Urban League of Cincinnati Records, Cincinnati History Library and Archives.

A bracketed date (e.g., [1965]) indicates the document is not formally dated but internal evidence argues for the date shown.

Page numbers given for *Cincinnati Enquirer* articles are those associated with their archival scans, not the pagination of the physical issue. Some archived newspaper clippings and reports accessed for this volume did not provide page numbers.

Adams, Patricia L. 1985. "Fighting for Democracy in St. Louis: Civil Rights during World War II." *Missouri Historical Review* 80, no. 1:58–75.

Aldridge, Kevin. 2001. "Race Task Force Adds Members." *Cincinnati Enquirer,* June 25, p. B1.

Anglen, Robert. 2000. "Director Hired, but City Council Has Reservations." *Cincinnati Enquirer,* February 25, p. D5.

———. 2000. "Race Agency Defends Work: Sees Politics in Critical Report." *Cincinnati Enquirer,* January 12, p. B1.

"Back on the Block, 1997." [1997]. ARBA (box not cataloged).

"Back on the Block." [2001]. ARBA (box not cataloged).

Black, Helen. 2014. Interview by Michael E. Maloney. Audio tape and transcript in possession of Maloney.

Black, Robert L., Jr. 1967. "Statement about McPheeters Report." Mimeo. ARBA, box 17.

Bragdon, Marshall. 1959. "Director's Monthly Report." July–August. ARBA, box 1.

———. [1965]. "MFRC 1943–1965: Story of the Mayor's Friendly Relations Committee of Cincinnati, Ohio, a Pioneer Intergroup Relations Agency." Mimeo. ARBS, box 2.

Brean, Herbert. 1957. "A Really Good Police Force." *Life,* September 16.

Bronson, Peter. 2007. "Improve Human Relations—on Council." *Cincinnati Enquirer,* February 1, p. 27.

Bruner, Borgna, and Elissa Haney. N.d. "Civil Rights Timeline: Milestones in the Modern Civil Rights Movement." http://www.infoplease.com/spot/civilrightstimeline1.html. Accessed November 3, 2015.

Burnham, Robert A. 1993. "The Mayor's Friendly Relations Committee: Cultural Pluralism and the Struggle for Black Advancement." In Taylor 1993, 258–79.

Christenson, Dorothy H. 2015. *Keep on Fighting: The Life and Civil Rights Legacy of Marian A. Spencer.* Athens: Ohio University Press.

"Chronicle of CHRC's Involvement on Racial Disturbance, April 4–12, 1968." [1968]. Unsigned, undated mimeo. ARBA, box 7.

Cincinnati Enquirer. 1944. "Walter White to Speak at Relations Institute." September 16, p. 8.

———. 1953. "Ordinance Urged in Report on Job Discrimination in City's Industry." April 14.

———. 1965. "Bragdon Honored for His Services." July 7, p. 3.

———. 1966. "Negroes Will Get Union Training." March 10, p. 28.

———. 1966. "Sparrow, Leaving Sees Race Progress." August 15, p. 31.

———. 1967. "Mayor Takes Reins of HR Group." December 31, p. 6.

———. 1967. "Riot Analyst's Pay Is Stopped—Till He Reports." October 20, p. 25.

———. 1968. "A New Role for the CHRC?" January 6, p. 4.

———. 1971. "Police Called Target for Black Frustrations." March 19.

———. 1972. "CHRC Members Are Furious over Staff Member's Arrest." July 1, p. 18.

———. 1975. "Auditor Rules against Funds for Mrs. Coffey." June 3, p. 14.

———. 1975. "Apology Asked of Ohio Auditor." June 14, p. 28.

———. 1978. "Alleged Luken Comment Charged to CHRC's Crum." May 13, p. 43.

———. 1978. "Brush Asks Council to Delay CHRC Report." March 16, p. 20.

———. 1978. "CHRC Tells Revision Ideas." May 13, p. 45.

———. 1978. "Helen Hinkley Would Have Been a Good Member." November 14, p. 12.

———. 1978. "Leistler Hits CHRC Tally of Charges." July 29, p. 1.

———. 1978. "Proposed Cut Upsets CHRC Chairman." November 9, p. 20.

———. 1978. "Revamp of CHRC Nears Approval." July 12, p. 27.

———. 1983. "Hall-Craig to Head CHRC." January 21, p. 34.

———. 1988. "Report Shows Incidence of Discrimination Rising." March 5, p. A12.

———. 1994. "Cincinnati Has 'a Lot of Willing Hearts' to Combat Racism." January 10, p. 6.

———. 2002. "Footnote." January 16, p. 12.

———. 2003. "Group Celebrates 60 Years as Human Relations Bridge." April 23, p. 20.

———. 2005. "Thomas Leaving Commission Post." July 6, p. 17.

———. 2006. "Norma Holt Davis Has Joined CHRC as Executive Director." May 22, p. 10.

———. 2007. "Chris Bortz Criticized over Call to City Official." February 21, p. 15.

———. 2007. "Neo-Nazis a No-Show, but Many Attended Rally to Support Peace." April 21, p. 14.

Cincinnati Herald. 1998. "Arzell Nelson Retires from CHRC." February 21, p. 1.

———. 2001. "CHRC's Future in City Council's Hands." May 13, p. 1.

———. 2007. "City Funding Decrease Could End Human Relations Work." January 26, p. A1.

———. 2011. "Meadows to Step Down as CHRC Executive Director." October 11, p. 1.

———. 2012. "CHRC Welcomes New Director." August 4, p. 1.

Cincinnati Human Relations Commission. 1944–65. Mayor's Friendly Relations Committee Meeting Minutes. ARBB, box 4.

―――. 1964–2009. Annual Reports. ARBA, box 10.

―――. 1965–68. Annual Reports. ARBA, box 7.

―――. 1971. Annual Report. ARBA, box 35.

―――. 1974–77. Annual Reports. ARBB, box 1.

―――. [1983]. "40 Years of Service to the Community." Unsigned, undated mimeo. ARBA, box 10.

―――. [1997]. "Chuck Harmon Fund File." ARBA (box not cataloged).

―――. 2012. "Cincinnati Human Relations Commission Welcomes New Executive Director." News release. https://docs .google.com/document/d/1k1EKmwmY7X9GITSphtpCN_ JFiOSWCK828lGbhLJA9os/edit. Accessed November 17, 2015.

―――. n.d. Commission Meeting Minutes. ARBB, box 5.

Cincinnati History Library and Archives. "Virginia Coffey, 1904– 2003." http://library.cincymuseum.org/aag/bio/coffey.html. Accessed August 29, 2015.

Cincinnati Human Relations Commission. 1972. "Appalachian Week in Review." *Human Relations Newsletter.* ARBA, box 35.

―――. 1975. "CHRC Answers State Auditor." *Human Relations Newsletter.* July.

―――. [2003]. "Cincinnati Youth Streetworkers Program, 2003." ARBA (box not cataloged).

Cincinnati Post. 1948. "Wage Boosts Proposed for Two." September 29.

―――. 1949. "Girl Scout Camp Opens to All Races." June 23.

―――. 1949. "Mayor's Friendly Group to 'Sell' Services to City." January 14.

―――. 1951. "Answering the Communists." January 2.

―――. 1951. "Woman Named to Head Race Relations Body." January 17.

―――. 1956. "State Questions Expenditures of Friendly Relations Committee." November 19.

―――. 1963. "City Human Relations Commission Is Urged." December 5.

―――. 1998. "Board Intact." June 10, p. 15.

―――. 2000. "Relations Commission Changing." December 7, p. 16.

Cincinnati Post and Times-Star. 1963. "At the City Club." January 17.

―――. 1963. "A Group at Work for Civic Harmony." April 20.

―――. 1968. "Revamp Plan for CHRC Submitted." January 31.

―――. 1968. "Ruehlmann Seeking Human Relations Format." January 2.

"Cincinnati Riots of 2001." https://en.wikipedia.org/wiki /Cincinnati riots of 2001. Accessed October 20, 2015.

City Beat. 2000. "Human Relations Commission Has New Director, but Where Will It Go from Here?" March 9. http://www.citybeat .com/home/article/13023827/human-relations-commission -has-new-director-but-where-will-it-go-from-here?" Accessed December 6, 2013.

City of Cincinnati. 2015. "An Ordinance Establishing the Office of Human Relations under the City Manager." Ordinance 397– 2015, adopted December 16.

"Civil Rights Movement 1980's–1990's." https://www.timetoast .com/timelines/civil-rights-movement-1980s-1990s. Accessed October 20, 2015.

Cleveland Call and Post. 1950. "Mayor's Committee to Mark Birthday." November 11.

———. 1954. "Invites 1,700 on February 3." January 30.

———. 1954. "Mayor's Committee Sponsors Workshop." October 9.

———. 1955. "Cites Work of Cincy Relations Committee." January 22.

———. 1958. "Trace 12 Year Effort to Build Friendly Relations." March 1.

———. 1963. "Relations Committee Strikes at Job Bias." August 17.

Clingman, Lewis. n.d. "The Balance Sheet." City of Grand Rapids, MI, Archive, Equal Opportunity Department's Community Relations Files, box 13.

———. n.d. "Moustache and Riot Produce Reorganization." City of Grand Rapids, MI, Archive, Equal Opportunity Department's Community Relations Files, box 13.

Cloud, Fred. n.d. "On the Case for 50 Years: A Brief History of the National Association of Human Rights Workers." https://www .nahrw.org/our-history. Accessed January 26, 2015.

Coffey, Virginia. 1961. "England's New Racial Problems and Remedial Efforts as Seen by an American Intergroup Specialist." Mimeo. CHLU, box 24.

———. 1969. "City Manager's Meeting at St. Edmund's Camp" (Memo to City Manager Richard Krabach). Mimeo. ARBA, box 7.

———. 1980. Interview by Adeline Harris. CHL. Mss AT, interview 10.

———. [1980]. Interview by Stephanie Corsbie. CHL. Cincinnati Women Working Audio Collection, Mss AT, interview 4.

———. 1990. Interview by Thomas E. Wagner. Audio tape and transcript in possession of Wagner.

Collins, William. 1957. "Our City's Problem—Migrant Mountaineer—Social Thorn or Economic Bulwark?" *Cincinnati Enquirer,* four-part series beginning July 14, p. 1.

"Council Defers Action on Move to Raise Pay." 1948. Newspaper clipping, CHLU, box 24.

"Council Votes to Weigh Offer." 1948. Newspaper clipping, CHLU, box 24.

Cudnik, Doreen. 2000. "Don't Criticize CHRC's Acting Director." *Cincinnati Enquirer,* Letters to the Editor. June 3, p. 7.

Curnutte, Mark. 1993. "A Polite Silence: Race Relations in Cincinnati." *Cincinnati Enquirer,* six-part series beginning November 21, p. 1.

Daily Mail. 2011. "One in Four Americans Feel Racial Relations Have Gotten Worse since Barack Obama Took Office." http://www .dailymail.co.uk/news/article. Accessed August 18, 2015.

Dam, Shubhankar. 2007. "Lessons from National Human Rights Institutions around the World for State and Local Human Rights Commissions in the United States." http://www.hks.harvard.edu /index.php/content/download/67465/1242670/version/1 /file/hri.pdf. Accessed January 26, 2015.

DiFillippo, Dana. 1996. "Panel Hears Requests for Gay-Rights Provisions." *Cincinnati Enquirer.* December 8, p. 30.

Dodson, Dan W. 1951. "Public Intergroup Relations Agencies." *Journal of Negro Education* 20, no. 3:398–407.

Donovan, Lisa. 1998. "Council May Revamp Group: CHRC Has Lost Focus, They Fear." *Cincinnati Enquirer,* June 22, p. 3.

———. 1998. "Hands Off Agency, Council Told." *Cincinnati Enquirer,* August 25, p. B2.

"Double Attendance Noted at Annual Relations Event." 1952. Newspaper clipping. ARBB, box 72.

Downey, Dennis J. 2006. "Elaborating Consensus: Strategic Orientations and Rationales in Wartime Intergroup Relations." *Mobilization: An International Quarterly* 11, no. 3:337–56.

Edwards, Carolyn. 2015. Interview by Michael E. Maloney. Audio tape and transcript in possession of Maloney.

Film and History Conference. 2004. "Linciati: Lynchings of Italians in America." Documentary film. http://www.uwosh.edu /filmandhistory/documentary/americanhistory1/linciati.php. Accessed February 10, 2015.

Find Law. "Civil Rights: Timeline of Events." http://civilrights .findlaw.com/civil-rights-overview/civil-rights-timeline-of-events .html. Accessed September 23, 2015.

Finkle, Lee. 1973. "The Conservative Aims of Militant Rhetoric: Black Protest during World War II." *Journal of American History* 60, no. 3:692–713.

"Friendly Relations Group Refused $1,000 Increase." 1948. Newspaper clipping, ARBB, box 72.

Garloch, Karen. 1982. "Garner Resigns Position." *Cincinnati Enquirer,* September 10, p. 29.

Garry, Patricia. 2015. Interview by Michael E. Maloney. Audio tape and transcript in possession of Maloney.

Goetz, Kristina. 2001. "Study Circles Program Unifies Law, Communities." *Cincinnati Enquirer,* June 25, p. 10.

Gonzalez-Day, Ken. 2006. *Lynching in the West, 1850–1935.* Durham: Duke University Press.

Good, Tedd. 2014. Interview by Michael E. Maloney. Audio tape and transcript in possession of Maloney.

Goodman, Rebecca. 2009. "Thomas L Garner Was City Peacemaker." *Cincinnati Enquirer,* March 28, p. 18.

Gregg, B. G. 1998. "Human Relations Head to End 25 Years of Service." *Cincinnati Enquirer,* February 14, p. B9.

Gusweiler, Mert. 1961. "Bragdon Sees Progress Made in Race Relations." *Cincinnati Enquirer,* April 6, p. 32.

Hahn, George, and David W. Reed. 1978. "Chief Leistler, FOP President Blast Criticism of Police in Wounding of City Employee." *Cincinnati Enquirer,* April 13, p. 17.

Harrington, Jeff. 1992. "Whitney to Resign from Commission." *Cincinnati Enquirer,* June 20, p. 22.

Harris, Robert. 2014. Interview by Michael E. Maloney. Audio tape and transcript in possession of Maloney.

Hirtl, Leo. 1949. "Judges, Police Absent from Anti-bigotry Parley." *Cincinnati Post,* January 14.

Hood, Camille. 1949. "Race Leaders Shy from Cincy Affair." *Pittsburgh Courier,* January [date illegible].

Howard, Allen. 1978. "Blacks Blast CHRC Appointment." *Cincinnati Enquirer,* December 5, p. 46.

———. 1978. "Budget Cut Seen Putting CHRC Near Extinction." *Cincinnati Enquirer,* December 19, p. 29.

———. 1978. "CHRC Power Crumbling, Garner Fears." *Cincinnati Enquirer,* May 7, p. 21.

———. 1978. "CHRC Role Subject of Upcoming Report." *Cincinnati Enquirer,* May 7, p. 17.

———. 1978. "CHRC Still Puzzling over Place of Sexual Preference Clause." *Cincinnati Enquirer*, April 23, p. 19.

———. 1978. "CHRC Vows Fund Cuts Won't End Its Housing Say." *Cincinnati Enquirer*, December 15, p. 29.

———. 1978. "Luken Denies He Wanted CHRC Abolished." *Cincinnati Enquirer*, May 12, p. 1.

———. 1978. "Possible CHRC Member Conflict Studied." *Cincinnati Enquirer*, June 9, p. 46.

———. 1978. "Questions, Objections Bog Down Plan to Restructure CHRC." *Cincinnati Enquirer*, May 17, p. 22.

———. 1978. "Staffer Fears Move to Weaken CHRC." *Cincinnati Enquirer*, May 7, p. 17.

———. 1986. "Tuning Human Relations." *Cincinnati Enquirer*, March 1, p. 8.

———. 1995. "Group Braves City Streets to Keep Peace." *Cincinnati Enquirer*, August 13, p. 146.

———. 1997. "Youths Dive into Scuba and Snorkeling at Pools." *Cincinnati Enquirer*, June 21, p. 17.

———. 2003. "Neighbors' Award Has an Opening." *Cincinnati Enquirer*, February 18, p. 11.

Howard, Allen, and Martin Hogan Jr. 1978. "Some Council Members Object to Council Votes." *Cincinnati Enquirer*, October 22, p. 21.

Howard, Allen, and Dave Reid. 1978. "City Housing Pacts May Go to HOME." *Cincinnati Enquirer*, May 2, p. 37.

"Immigration Act of 1924." http://en.wikipedia.org/wiki /Immigration_Act_of_1924. Accessed February 10, 2015

Johnson, Charles D. 2015. "Marshall Bragdon papers, 1923–1981." amistadresearchcenter.tulane.edu/archon/?p=collections /controlcard&id=215. (Note: This is a two-step link.) Accessed August 26, 2015.

Josten, Margaret. 1957. "Little Rock Strife? That Is Reason for Friendly Relations Endeavors." *Cincinnati Enquirer*, September 12.

———. 1968. "Commission: 'Inhumanity Out; Quiet Progress In.'" *Cincinnati Enquirer*, November 25, p. 1.

———. 1968. "'New Image' for CHRC Revealed." *Cincinnati Enquirer*, January 3.

———. 1977. "Two More Human Relations Commissioners Angrily Resign." *Cincinnati Enquirer*, March 5, p. 38.

———. 1978. "CHRC Services May Overlap Other Agencies." *Cincinnati Enquirer*, January 7, p. 33.

Kalish, Jim. 2000. *The Story of Civil Rights in York, Pennsylvania: A 250 Year Interpretive History.* York, PA: York County Audit of Human Rights.

King-Betts, Ericka. 2016. Telephone interview by Phillip J. Obermiller. Notes on this conversation in possession of Obermiller.

Klepal, Dan, and Cindi Andrews. 2001. "Stories of 15 Black Men Killed by Police since 1995." *Cincinnati Enquirer,* April 15, p. 18A.

Kornbluh, Andrea Tuttle. 1986. *Lighting the Way: The Woman's City Club of Cincinnati, 1915–1965.* Cincinnati: Woman's City Club.

———. 1986. "Woman's City Club: A Pioneer in Race Relations." *Queen City Heritage,* Summer, pp. 21–38.

Krieger, Dave. 1978. "Chances for Proposed Rights Ordinance Doubtful." *Cincinnati Enquirer,* April 15, p. 39.

———. 1978. "Revisions Delay Rights Proposal." *Cincinnati Enquirer,* May 25, p. 83.

———. 1979. "Donaldson Attacks City's Human Relations Panel." *Cincinnati Enquirer,* March 17, p. 45.

———. 1979. "More Black Policemen Would Help, CHRC Says." *Cincinnati Enquirer,* March 16, p. 25.

Larson, Erik. 2011. *In the Garden of Beasts.* New York: Crown (esp. pp. 29–32).

Leadership Conference. 2015. "Civil Rights 101: Civil Rights Chronology." http://www.civilrights.org/resources/civilrights101/chronology.html. Accessed October 20, 2015.

Leonard, Thomas. C. 2016. *Illiberal Reformers: Race, Eugenics, and American Economics in the Progressive Era.* Princeton: Princeton University Press.

Levy, Burton. 1971. "The Bureaucracy of Race: Enforcement of Civil Rights Laws and Its Impact on People, Process, and Organization." *Journal of Black Studies* 2, no. 1:77–105.

Lieberman, Robbie, and Clarence Lang, eds. 2009. *Anticommunism and the African American Freedom Movement: Another Side of the Story.* New York: Palgrave Macmillan.

"List of Ethnic Riots." http://en.wikipedia.org/wiki/List_of_ethnic_riots. Accessed January 10, 2015.

"List of Strikes." http://en.wikipedia.org/wiki/List_of_strikes#1900s. Accessed January 10, 2015.

"Los Angeles Riots." 1992. https://en.wikipedia.org/wiki/1992_Los_Angeles_riots. Accessed October 21, 2015.

Lynch, Rev. Damon, Jr. 2014. Interview by Michael E. Maloney. Audio tape and transcript in possession of Maloney.

Maloney, Michael E. 1974. *The Social Areas of Cincinnati: Toward an Analysis of Social Needs.* Cincinnati Human Relations Commission.

———. 1986. *The Social Areas of Cincinnati: An Analysis of Social Needs.* Cincinnati Human Relations Commission.

"Mass Racial Violence in the United States." https://en.wikipedia .org/wiki/Mass_racial_violence_in_the_United_States#Jim _Crow_period:_1890.E2.80.931914. Accessed February 27, 2015.

May, Lucy. 1998. "CHRC Board Out en Masse." *Cincinnati Enquirer,* June 26, p. C1.

Mayo, Harry. 1954. "The 'Ways' of Mountain Folk in City." *Cincinnati Post,* September 20.

McClung, Lori. 1993. "Fight Spurs Talks in Lower Price Hill." *Cincinnati Post,* December 29, p. 9A.

McLarty, Scott. 2014. Interview by Michael E. Maloney. Audio tape and transcript in possession of Maloney.

McPheeters, David D., Jr. [1966]. "A Proposed Plan to Prevent Riots." Mimeo. ARBA, box 17.

———. [1967]. Untitled report on the 1967 riots in Cincinnati. Mimeo. ARBA, box 17.

———. 2014. Interview by Michael E. Maloney, Geoff Daniels, and Charles F. Casey-Leninger. Audio tape and transcript in possession of Maloney.

Meadows, Cheryl. 2014. Interview by Michael E. Maloney. Audio tape and transcript in possession of Maloney.

MFRC. Articles of Incorporation of the Mayor's Friendly Relations Committee. 1949. CHLU, box 24.

———. 1963. "Executive Director's Report for March." ARBB, box 67.

———. 1964. "Presentation to Council Welfare Committee." CHLU, box 24.

Milam, Brett. 2016. "Remembering 1979, When Cincinnati Cops Weren't Safe." *Cincinnati Enquirer,* July 24, p. 2AA.

Miller, Martha. 1991. "Dorothy Dolbey, Civic Leader." *Cincinnati Enquirer,* February 14, p. 42.

Mjagkij, Nina. 1993. "Behind the Scenes: The Cincinnati Urban League, 1948–63." In Taylor 1993, 280–94.

Moyn, Samuel. 2010. *The Last Utopia: Human Rights in History.* Cambridge, MA: Belknap Press.

Negro Organizations Interested in Racial Amity and Good City
    Government. 1943. "Statement." CHLU, box 24.
Nelson, Arzell. 2014. Interview by Michael E. Maloney. Audio tape
    and transcript in possession of Maloney.
Noonan, Susan. 2014. Interview by Michael E. Maloney. Audio tape
    and transcript in the possession of Maloney.
Obermiller, Phillip J., and Thomas E. Wagner. 2000. "Cincinnati's
    'Second Minority': The Emergence of Appalachian Advocacy,
    1953–1973." In *Appalachian Odyssey: Historical Perspectives on the
    Great Migration*, ed. Obermiller, Wagner, and E. Bruce Tucker,
    193–214. Westport, CT: Praeger.
Osborn, Kevin. 2000. "Council to Decide Human Relations
    Commission's Fate." *Cincinnati Post*, January 27.
———. 2000. "Human Relations Vote Blocked: Reece Wants Vote on
    Agency's Fate." *Cincinnati Post*, February 17, p. 14.
Oshinsky, David. 2016. "No Justice for the Weak." *New York Times Book
    Review*, March 20, p. 1.
Posner, Eric A. 2014. *The Twilight of Human Rights Law*. New York:
    Oxford University Press.
Ransohof, Jerry. 1954. "Budget Tables Bid for Furniture, So City
    Official Builds His Own." *Cincinnati Post*, January 25.
Redding, Barbara. 1978. "Blackwell Sees CHRC as Investigatory
    Unit." *Cincinnati Enquirer*, February 27, p. 21.
———. 1978. "CHRC Hot Over Plans for Funds." *Cincinnati Enquirer*,
    May 1, p. 39.
Reid, David W. 1978. "Answers Elude Council on Some Tough
    Issues." *Cincinnati Enquirer*, November 26, p. 17.
Roman, Al. 1949. "Roman the Valley." *Cleveland Call and Post*,
    September 3.
———. 1952. "Roaming the Valley with Roman." *Cincinnati Herald*,
    July 12.
———. 1956. "Cincinnati Listening Post." *Cleveland Call and Post*,
    February 4.
Rucker, Walter C., and James N. Upton. 2007. *Encyclopedia of American
    Race Riots*. 2 vols. Westport, CT: Greenwood.
Sanger, Carol. 1973. "A Lot Has Changed for Human Relations
    Panel." *Cincinnati Post*, November 12, p. 13.
Saunders, Kenneth L., and Hyo Eun Bang. 2007. "A Historical
    Perspective on U.S. Human Rights Commissions." http://www
    .hks.harvard.edu/index.php/content/download/67468

/1242682/version/1/file/history_of_hrc.pdf. Accessed February 11, 2015.

Schottlekotte, Al. 1957. "Cincinnati Racial Relations." *Cincinnati Enquirer,* October 25, p. 7.

Sitkoff, Harvard. 1971. "Racial Militancy and Interracial Violence in the Second World War." *Journal of American History* 58, no. 3:661–81.

Smith, Janet E. [1949]. "The First Five Years of the Mayor's Friendly Relations Committee, 1943–1948." Mimeo. ARBA, box 10.

Smitherman, Barbara. 2014. Interview by Michael E. Maloney. Audio tape and transcript in possession of Maloney.

Sowders, Kathleen. 1972. "The Festival—An Observation." *Human Relations Newsletter,* CHRC. ARBA, box 35.

Spencer, David. 1972. "Appalachian Conference Report." *Human Relations Newsletter,* CHRC. ARBA, box 35.

Spencer, Marian. 2014. Interview by Michael E. Maloney. Audio tape and transcript in possession of Maloney.

Spiegel, S. Arthur. 1965. Letter to Herbert R. Bloch Jr. ARBB, box 67.

———. 1996. Interview by Thomas E. Wagner. Audio tape and transcript in the possession of Wagner.

———. 2009. *A Trial on Its Merits: The Life of a Federal Judge.* Cincinnati: Clerisy Press.

"Study Completed on Mountaineers." 1954. *New York Times,* October 10.

Sturmon, Sarah. 1998. "Human Relations Board Resigns in Mass Protest." *Cincinnati Post,* June 26.

———. 1998. "Lost in City Hall: $480,000 Agency: Human Relations Mission, Future Both under Review." *Cincinnati Post,* July 20, p. 8A.

———. 1998. "A Struggle to Redo Old Rights Committee." *Cincinnati Post,* August 25, p. 9A.

Sullivan, Gary. 1978. "Brush Will Unveil Plan for Overhauling CHRC." *Cincinnati Enquirer,* May 8, p. 41.

Taylor, Henry Louis, Jr., ed. *Race and the City: Work, Community, and Protest in Cincinnati, 1820–1970.* Urbana: University of Illinois Press.

Thomas, Cecil. 2002. Letter to Whom It May Concern. May 28. ARBB, box 36.

———. 2014. "Interview by Michael E. Maloney." Audio tape and transcript in possession of Maloney.

———. N.d. Message from the executive director. ARBA, box 11.

"Transcription of Remarks at a Meeting of CHRC Concerning the History of the Commission." [1971]. ARBA, box 12.

Tucker, Randy. 2001. "'Study Circles' Project under Way." *Cincinnati Enquirer,* September 25, p. 14.

University of Missouri–Kansas City, School of Law. "Lynchings: By State and Race, 1882–1968." http://law2.umkc.edu/faculty /projects/ftrials/shipp/lynchingsstate.html. Accessed February 10, 2015.

U.S. Department of Justice. 2003. "Guidelines for Effective Human Relations Commissions." http://www.justice.gov/archive/crs /pubs/gehrc.pdf. Accessed January 25, 2016.

Vela, Susan. 2001. "Official Takes Pulse of OTR." *Cincinnati Enquirer,* May 14, p. B1.

Vogel v. City of Cincinnati, 9599 F2d 594, http://openjurist .org/959/f2d/594/vogel-v-city-of-cincinnati. Accessed October 1, 2015.

Wagner, Thomas E., and Phillip J. Obermiller. 1999. *Valuing Our Past, Creating Our Future: The Founding of the Urban Appalachian Council.* Berea, KY: Berea College Press.

Walker, Arnold B. 1943. "Will There Be a Race Riot in Cincinnati?" Division of Negro Welfare Bulletin, Council of Social Agencies, Cincinnati Community Chest. Mimeo. ARBA, box 24.

Weaver, Robert C. 1944. "Whither Northern Race Relations Committees?" *Phylon* 5, no. 3:216.

"We Shall Be Resolute." [1944]. Mimeo. CHLU, box 24.

Wilson, Denise. 1990. "City Project Aims to Provide a Safe Summer." *Cincinnati Post,* March 28, p. 14.

Winston, Earnest. 2001. "Play with a Purpose: Police, Firefighters, Youth Relax in Park." *Cincinnati Enquirer,* June 23, p. 13.

Index

Page numbers in italics refer to pages with photographs.

INDEX